Jazz Survivor

For Emily, Harry and Dorothy
And for Flora

'If I'm feeling tomorrow like I feel today
I'll pack my trunk and make my getaway.'

St. Louis Blues, by W. C. Handy

Jazz Survivor

The Story of Louis Bannet,
Horn Player of Auschwitz

Ken Shuldman

VALLENTINE MITCHELL
LONDON • PORTLAND, OR

First published in 2005 in Great Britain by
VALLENTINE MITCHELL
Suite 314, Premier House,
112–114 Station Road,
Edgware, Middlesex HA8 7BJ
and in the United States of America by
VALLENTINE MITCHELL
c/o ISBS, 920 NE 58th Avenue, Suite 300
Portland, Oregon, 97213-3786

Website http://www.vmbooks.com

British Library Cataloging in Publication Data:

A catalogue record for this book is available
from the British Library

ISBN 0-85303-476-1

Library of Congress Cataloging-in-Publication Data:

A catalog record for this book is available
from the Library of Congress

Printed in Great Britain by
Antony Rowe Ltd, Chippenham, Wiltshire

Contents

Plates

Acknowledgements

This was not a journey I embarked upon alone, and I'd like to acknowledge those who traveled by my side, both physically and spiritually. To my wife Emily and our children, Harry and Dorothy. Thank you for your love and understanding, and for always lifting my spirits. To my Aunt Sylvia Tobias and my brother Steve for sharing your faith, your kitchen, and your love of tradition. To my dear departed friend Sandy Corbet, who thought 'this trumpet guy' would be a great and important story to tell. To Jeroen Bours: we both lost our fathers when we were young, but then we found Louis and became brothers. This story is our story. To my dear friends in Toronto, Marnie and Steven and Irene Loewy, thank you for the many kindnesses, and for your love and support. To Louis Bannet Jr., for allowing me to be a part of your family. To Dr Jud Newborn for discovering Louis Bannet and bringing him into the lives of so many. To my friends at the Museum of Jewish Heritage/A Living Memorial to the Holocaust, thank you for keeping hope and memory alive. To Rabbi Stuart Gershon and Shyalpa Rinpoche, your spiritual messages came through loud and clear. To Emma Fialka for bringing your heart and soul to Louis. And to Billy Altman, Vincent Cariello, Cheryl Gackstetter, Hans Vanderwerff, Ray Benjamin, James Salzano, and K. J. Bowen, for helping me complete the journey. Most of all, this book would not have been possible without Flora.

Introduction

We drew up in ranks of five, with the musicians. They were nearly all Jews: Juliek, a bespectacled Pole with a cynical smile on his pale face; Louis, a distinguished musician who came from Holland – he complained that they would not let him play Beethoven: Jews were not allowed to play German music.

From *Night* by Elie Wiesel

Several years ago, a friend visited the Nazi death camp at Auschwitz-Birkenau. Standing alone near the site of where the crematoriums once stood, he heard the sound of a bird singing. How odd, he thought, to hear such a sweet sound in such a place.

Louis Bannet, the 'Louis' mentioned in Elie Wiesel's masterpiece of Holocaust literature, was like that bird.

Jazz Survivor is the remarkable tale of a Dutch Jewish trumpet star who became known as the Dutch Louis Armstrong, a man who blew the Nazis away.

In his life, Louis Bannet played for kings and queens, monsters and madmen, and somehow survived the hell of all hells to become a renowned bandleader and host of one of Canada's most beloved television shows. It's a story that includes encounters with a colorful cast of historical figures, such as the legendary jazz saxophone player Coleman Hawkins, the French singing star Edith Piaf, Josef Mengele, and Louis Armstrong himself. Ultimately, though, it is a story about the power of music. As Louis Bannet said, 'I was stronger than Hitler – I could do whatever I wanted, as long as I had my trumpet in my hand.' Today that trumpet, a musical testament to survival, is on display at the Museum of Jewish Heritage/A Living Memorial to the Holocaust in New York City.

Prologue

I arrived early for Louis Bannet's memorial service that sweltering June day back in 2002. As I entered the Benjamin Funeral Home in Toronto, there were only a few people seated in the sanctuary, mostly older members of the Dutch community that once flourished in Toronto. These men and women, with their walkers and canes, had once danced to the driving rhythms of Louis Bannet and his band.

Sitting alone by the simple wooden coffin, silently reciting from the Book of Psalms, was the Shomer, the religious watchman and guardian of the spirit. I wondered, was one Shomer enough for such a spirit?

I first heard the name Louis Bannet while on a tour of the construction site of the Museum of Jewish Heritage/A Living Memorial to the Holocaust in New York City. At the time, I was working for the advertising agency that was developing a campaign for the museum. Dr David Altshuler, the museum's esteemed first director, was pointing to where several exhibits were to be displayed. As we gingerly walked past steel girders and exposed wires, he motioned towards a corner where a glass case would stand. Inside that case, he said, would be a trumpet that belonged to a man named Louis Bannet, once known as the Dutch Louis Armstrong. The idea of a trumpet and jazz in a Holocaust Museum seemed odd and strangely out of place, and I filed the story away in my memory.

About a year after the museum opened, I was asked to create several television commercials that would feature the great actress Meryl Streep and the violin virtuoso Itzhak Perlman, who were both providing the voices for the museum's audio tour. We decided that one commercial would feature Louis Bannet's story, and we flew him to New York from his home in Toronto. When he arrived on the set, we knew we were in the presence of someone very special. He began performing immediately, as if the last fifty years were just a brief intermission, and, in a matter of moments, he had everyone under his spell. But soon the magic would come face to face with the tragic. We had planned to use Louis' trumpet in the commercial, but the museum was concerned about its safety, so a production designer found an exact replica. Louis was brought to the second floor of the museum, the Holocaust floor. As you enter the room, you are greeted by a tiled wall of faces, gaunt with eyes sunk in their sockets. As Louis walked in, holding the trumpet, he met the gaze of the faces on the wall, the same people who may have heard his music as they were marched to the gas chambers. It was too much for him to bear. He fell to his knees and began to wail. Many in the crew of burly teamsters wept openly. Louis was helped up and, without missing a beat, said, 'Let's get to work.' The next thing we knew, he was sitting on Meryl Streep's lap.

During lunch he began to talk about some of his experiences before the war and in the camps. It seemed like he had one amazing story after another. It became quite clear that there was more to Louis Bannet's life than a thirty-second commercial.

Historian and lecturer Dr Jud Newborn, who originally brought Louis' trumpet to the museum, and accompanied him that day from his home in Toronto, characterized the day's events this way: 'The filming of that commercial was the fulfillment for him of his story – the culmination of the whole process of personal grief, letting go, feeling it all in vain – and then finally moving into collective history and memory for real, after all those years, knowing he really had borne witness in museum form after all.'

Over the next two years, together with my partner, Dutch translator and dearest friend Jeroen Bours, I made several trips to Toronto, interviewing Louis in his small music-filled study. Entering the Bannet home was like walking into a piece of Delft pottery. Everywhere you looked, everywhere you turned, there was blue – even in the bathroom, which was stocked with blue towels, blue tissue paper and blue soap. Those visits with Louis and his beloved Flora were filled with tears and laughter, as well as ample portions of brown bread, herring and *stroopwafels*, the Dutch caramel cookies Louis loved so. These were some of the most special moments in my life. And after each remarkable episode, Louis would turn to Jeroen and me and say, 'I tell you some stories, don't I, boys?'

This book is a humble attempt to give those stories a well-deserved home.

1. Young Louis

If you booked a room today on the second floor of the sprawling Hilton Hotel in Rotterdam, you'd be standing very close to the spot where Louis Bannet was born on 15 August 1911 at number 26 Kattendrecht. Today, this part of the city is a thriving business center. But in the early 1900s, it was a poor Jewish working-class neighborhood, the 'Lower East Side' of Rotterdam', known as the Helmersstraat.

Louis Bannet, born Levi Bannet, was the youngest son of Leon and Leenjte Bannet. At one time there were eight Bannet children, but a sister and two brothers died before Louis was born. When Louis came into the world most of his older siblings had already left home, so it was just Louis and his older brother Isaac who remained with their parents in the small two-room apartment.

Leon Bannet, Louis's father, was a mostly out-of-work fix-it man and an alcoholic, who at times could be abusive to his wife and children. Louis's mother Leentje (pronounced Leen-cha) like many women in poor families, was the sturdy rock of the household. She earned some money as a seamstress, but also relied on the generosity of her brother, Abraham van Beuren, who managed a blanket warehouse in Rotterdam.

Louis Bannet's first encounter with music took place when he was six years old. A neighbor in the building had a young son who practiced his violin at all hours of the day. Leentje would always find Louis sitting on the floor outside the apartment, ear pressed against the door. Unfortunately, although the boy practiced constantly, his lack of musical ability was painfully evident to everyone in the building.

One morning the boy's father opened his door and found Louis sitting in his usual spot. He told Louis to wait, and walked back into his apartment. A moment later he returned, violin in hand. Without saying a word, he handed Louis the worn violin and tattered bow,

1

smiled, and retreated behind the door. I assume the neighbors were quite happy, but not as happy as young Louis Bannet.

Call it a gift from God, call it a blessing, whatever it was, Louis possessed it, and by the time he was seven he had taught himself to play the violin.

Leentje Bannet loved to hear her son play. She knew he had a special talent, and longed for him to get professional training. Her husband had other thoughts. He believed music was a waste of time, and that money was better spent on other things, which for him meant alcohol. But every week, Leentje put away small amounts of money for Louis' musical education in a glass jar she kept hidden in a kitchen closet.

One warm spring day Louis was practicing a Beethoven piece in his room. The window, which faced the busy street, was wide open. Leon Bloorman, a German Jew, was walking past on his way to work. The sound he heard stopped him in his tracks. He looked up to see where the music was coming from, but couldn't see anything. He walked into the building and climbed the stairs, following the sound until he reached the Bannet apartment. He knocked on the door and was greeted by Leentje. He introduced himself and told her that he was a violin teacher at the Jewish Conservatory of Music. Leentje invited the young man inside to meet Louis. Bloorman, who was nearly forty years old, bent down and shook Louis' hand. He was astonished at the sight of his violin: he couldn't believe that such a beautiful tone could come from an instrument in such a terrible condition. He asked Louis to play for him, and again Louis played the Beethoven piece. When he had finished, Bloorman asked Leentje to bring Louis to the Conservatory the very next day to audition for the headmaster.

That night Louis practiced into the early morning hours. While he played, his mother sat in the kitchen worrying about how she would pay for her son's tuition should he be accepted.

The next morning, Louis and his mother made the short journey to the Conservatory. Leon Bloorman, holding a violin case, was waiting at the door. He escorted them down the hall to the headmaster's office. Once inside, he opened the violin case and asked Louis to take the violin in his hand. Louis lifted the instrument to his shoulder and began to pluck at the strings. He quickly placed it back in the case and reached for his own violin, still wrapped in the cloth case his

2

mother had made. He told Bloorman that he would prefer to use his own instrument. The headmaster entered the room and Bloorman introduced him to Louis and his mother. The headmaster asked a few questions, then asked Louis to play. Louis, without any sheet music, began to play an excerpt from Beethoven's violin concerto. The headmaster listened intently as Leentje and Bloorman gazed quietly at Louis. Moments later, the headmaster told Louis to stop playing, then asked him to wait outside with his mother while he conferred with Bloorman. After several minutes, the door opened and Louis and Leentje were told to come back in. The headmaster said he was very impressed with Louis' playing and thought that he could certainly benefit from some form of musical education, but he was concerned how such a young boy would cope in the competitive environment of the Conservatory. He said that he would admit Louis under one condition: if Mr Bloorman would personally take him under his musical tutelage, he would be allowed to attend the Conservatory. Bloorman readily agreed.

After the audition at the Conservatory, Louis had one more audition to attend. With his mother he went to the home of his uncle, Abraham von Beuren, to ask for help with tuition. Once again, Louis played the Beethoven piece. Uncle Abraham was very impressed with Louis' progress, having heard him play only at holiday parties. He agreed to help pay for Louis' tuition, and Louis promised his mother to use his musical talent to pay his uncle back.

At the Conservatory, Louis soon became one of the star pupils, and his ability as a leader of musicians also became apparent. Most of the students were also from poor families, so the need for additional income was always important. In his second year Louis formed a small orchestra with several students, and they hired themselves out for weddings and bar mitzvahs. Many, including Louis, weren't even of bar mitzvah age yet. They would also perform on street corners, with Louis passing a hat for contributions.

Whatever money Louis earned – and in those days it was considerable – went straight into the jar his mother kept hidden in the kitchen. This extra money helped keep the lights on for weeks on end. Of course, Bloorman was not particularly thrilled that some of his best students were playing music in the streets, but as long as they kept up with their practicing he never interfered.

Louis practiced constantly. Leon Greenman, a fellow survivor and

2. Pimps and Whores, Laurel and Hardy

According to Jewish law and tradition, thirteen-year-old Louis Bannet was now a man.

But on the streets of Rotterdam, he still wore short pants and leggings just like any other Dutch boy. This didn't stop him from taking to the streets to look for work as a professional musician, however. He had heard from some older students at the Conservatory of a place down by the waterfront called Charlie Stock's, a coffee house that doubled as a musician's hiring hall. When he walked in carrying his violin case, he was probably too young to realize that musicians weren't the only professionals available for hire at Charlie Stock's. The place was filled with merchant seamen, Chinese laborers, musicians, many with their instruments spread out on tables, and women: women unlike any he had seen in the Helmerstraat. Their faces were painted with lipstick and rouge. Their dresses were brightly coloured, not the drab blacks and grays worn by his Jewish neighbors, and there was much skin on display. As Louis attempted to venture further into the crowded hall, he was stopped by a man who told him that minors were not allowed inside. As he was being escorted out, he caught the attention of a young man sitting at a table playing cards with several young women. He motioned for the man to bring the young boy over.

'Aren't you a little young to be in a place like this?' the man asked.

'I heard from some friends at school that this was the place for musicians to find work,' Louis answered.

'This is a place for a lot people to find work,' the man said, looking around at the table of women. 'My name is Hein Frank. And who are you?'

'My name is Louis Bannet, and I play the violin.'

'Well, Louis Bannet, if you plan on finding work here, I can tell you one thing: Charlie Stock doesn't hire young boys. Come with me and we'll at least try to make you look the part.' (When Louis recounted this story for the first time for me, he was well into his eighties, and he was a little shy about admitting that Hein Frank was a pimp – and not just any pimp, he said, but a Jewish pimp.) Hein Frank took Louis to the back of the hall and down a long corridor past several rooms, all with their doors shut. Louis could hear the sound of men and women moaning and furniture creaking as he walked past the rooms. Hein opened the door to one of the rooms, quickly walked in, and in a few seconds came out with a pair of pants. He held them up to Louis and then asked him to try them on for size.

Louis slipped into the room to change, and walked out a man.

He didn't get any work that first day, nor did he find any on the second or third. But he came back day after day, and quickly learned how the selection process worked. It seemed that Charlie Stock always chose the same people. When he asked Hein Frank about this, Hein said Charlie had a very simple credo: you pay, you play. Sensing Louis' frustration, Hein paid Charlie Stock a visit; the next day, when a violin player was needed for a children's birthday party, Louis got the job.

He had to wait weeks, though, to be called again. But when he was finally chosen, he was sent to a cinema to play in the orchestra as silent movies from America played on the screen. Louis loved this job because it allowed him to play all types of music with a group of accomplished musicians. He played for cowboy movies, swashbuckling pirate adventures and tear-jerking melodramas. His favorites, though, were the comedies, especially Laurel and Hardy. There was just one problem. Louis couldn't stop laughing, and finally the theatre manager had to fire him because his laughter was distracting the other musicians. 'He said to me, "I hired you to play, not laugh,"' Louis recalled nearly eighty years later.

He returned again to Charlie Stock's, but new work rarely came his way. Louis couldn't understand why it was so hard to get work. Eventually, Hein Frank hired him to do some bookkeeping.

How Charlie Stock's came to be the place where Rotterdam's musicians went to find work, Louis was never certain. What is certain is that it was a gathering place for the sailors and dockworkers who unloaded the ships that arrived from all over the world. One thing the sailors always seemed to have with them was music, especially phonograph records from London and America. Charlie Stock played these records on a player he kept on the bar, and the sailors danced to the music with Hein Frank's girls. In fact, it was on one of those records that Louis first heard the music that would change his life.

'I was sitting in Hein Frank's office one day and I heard a sound that practically lifted me off my chair. I went out to the main hall and noticed a group of sailors standing by the record player. They were drinking and snapping their fingers to the music. I had never heard anything like it. I thought it was a trumpet, but I wasn't sure, since I'd never heard a trumpet sound like that. The notes were bending and moving in all different directions. There was a drumbeat pounding out a driving rhythm. I saw the record cover on the table and written on it was the name Louis Armstrong.'

As the weeks and months passed, Louis' prospects dimmed. Hein Frank had a simple explanation.

'Louis, look around you. All you see are violin cases. There are probably more violin players in Holland than tulips. Have you ever thought of another instrument?' he asked.

'This is the only instrument I know,' Louis answered. 'But maybe it's time to think of something new.'

Louis knew Hein Frank was right. But how could he tell his mother that he was giving up the violin?

Later that night, Louis lay awake in his bed waiting for his older brother Isaac to return from work. Isaac Bannet worked for their Uncle Abraham at his blanket factory. When he came home, he walked into the room, sat on the bed beside Louis' and removed his shoes.

'Isaac, I'm going to give up the violin,' Louis announced.

'What do you mean, give it up?' Isaac replied.

'There are too many violin players in this city and not enough jobs,' Louis answered.

'But what about all the years you spent at the Conservatory? What will Professor Bloorman say? What will our mother say?'

'That's why I'm doing it, for our mother, Isaac. I have to find a way to make more money so we can have more food on the table, so we can pay the rent, so the lights are not turned off every week.'

'What will you play?' Isaac asked.

'Maybe a saxophone, I'm not sure. All I know is that I need 30 guilders for a new instrument.'

'I'm sure Uncle Abraham would help you,' Isaac said. 'You should go and see him tomorrow.'

The next day Louis went to see his Uncle Abraham. When he walked on to the factory floor, the noise was deafening. As he walked passed the huge cutting tables, he saw his brother Isaac, who motioned him to climb the stairs to his uncle's office on the second floor. Louis entered the office. His uncle was stooped over his desk, eating a bowl of soup and reading from a Hebrew prayer book.

'My uncle was a very religious man,' Louis recalled. 'I tried to explain my problem to him, and I told him about the saxophone, but it seemed like he didn't hear me. Finally, he put his spoon down and closed his book. 'A saxophone,' he said. 'That's not a very Jewish instrument.' I told him that it had a shape like a Shofar. He reached into a desk drawer and pulled out a box. He opened it and counted out the thirty guilders. Before I left, he made me promise not to forget my violin, which I never did.'

Later that week, Louis went to Bommel's Music Store. Even after more than seventy years, Louis remembered this visit quite vividly.

'The walls of the music store were covered with a symphony's worth of instruments. Mr Bommel, he had a terrible stutter, and when I came into his store with all this money he was very surprised. I asked him what kind of saxophone could I buy with thirty guilders. He said I couldn't buy any saxophone with just thirty guilders. "Then what can I buy?" I asked. Mr Bommel walked to the end of the counter and reached for a trumpet. He said "For thirty guilders this is all I can offer you. Do you know how to play?" I took the trumpet and brought it to my lips and blew, but I couldn't make a sound. He said "Your lips are cold – rub them with the back of your hand like this," and he showed me how.

So I rubbed my lips and again brought the trumpet to my mouth and I blew, and I made a loud sound that frightened some of the other people in the store. Mr Bommel said I had a healthy set of lungs, and he said one day people would pay to hear me play.'

As with the violin, Louis Bannet took to the trumpet quickly, and, thanks again to the generosity of his Uncle Abraham, he was able to study with a well-known teacher, Aaron DeVries, the patriarch of a very well-respected Dutch musical family. He also had another teacher – Louis Armstrong. Every chance he got, he would head down to Charlie Stock's or one of the many music shops in

Rotterdam and listen to Louis Armstrong and his Hot Five. One of the recordings he listened to over and over was the 1925 recording of *St. Louis Blues*, with the legendary Bessie Smith on vocals. He memorized it note for note, and practiced it so much that his neighbors must have thought they were living on Bourbon Street and not Katendrecht.

In 1929, as the world's economy was about to tumble, Louis Bannet landed his first trumpet gig with a novelty jazz band called Anton Swan and the Swantockers. Anton Swan, a tall, lanky Dutchman more interested in getting laughs then getting people on the dance floor, dressed the band in silly sailor suits and fake mustaches. But he was smart enough to realize that in Louis Bannet he had a first-rate soloist who could play any song the audience requested. And as the band started playing the dance halls and clubs in Amsterdam and The Hague, the signs outside now read Anton Swan and the Swantockers, featuring Louis Bannet on trumpet.

3. All That Jazz

When the great tenor saxophonist Coleman Hawkins left Fletcher Henderson's band in New York and headed for Europe towards the tail end of 1934 he was like Louis Bannet, searching for a new musical environment. Arriving at the port of Rotterdam aboard the *Ile de France*, he had no idea what to expect from the Dutch jazz scene – in fact, he wasn't sure if one even existed. But in truth, jazz was all the rage in Holland. Groups like the Ramblers, the Bouncers, the Swing Papas, and the Red, White, and Blue Aces were in full swing by the time Hawkins reached port. Though never quite approaching the level of play of their American heroes, many Dutch jazz musicians fared quite well, and what they lacked in 'chops' they made up with heart and humor.

The arrival of Coleman Hawkins in Holland was big news for jazz musicians and jazz fans. One of those young fans was an aspiring trumpet player and close friend of Louis Bannet's, Pieter Dolk. Pieter knew that Louis was growing restless playing with the frivolous Anton Swan, so one night he took him to see 'The Hawk', Coleman Hawkins, at the Lido in Amsterdam. As Louis remembered, 'Just about every jazz musician in Holland was there that night, many hoping to sit in.' Hawkins ripped through a long set that included rousing renditions of *Honeysuckle Rose*, *Avalon*, and *Stardust*. For his encore, Hawkins announced to the crowd that he was going to play *Tiger Rag*, and invited any musician who wanted to play up to the stage. The first one to hit the stage was a Dutch drummer named Maurits von Kleef. Following right behind him was an extremely nervous Louis Bannet. Louis took a short, but spirited, solo. Drummer von Klaaf tore into his skins and brought the Dutch crowd to its feet. After the set, Louis and Maurits went back to Hawkins' dressing room. They jammed a little, but mostly talked and listened, as Hawkins regaled them with stories about some of the great players he had known. As a show of Dutch hospitality, Maurits introduced Hawkins to a Dutch drink made with egg yolks and brandy. Louis distinctly remembered that Hawkins' second set was not as sharp as his first.

But that night was important for one other reason. It was the beginning of an enduring friendship. Louis had found a kindred spirit in Maurits von Kleef, as well as someone who could supply the backbeat to a band of his own. Over the next several months Louis auditioned musicians from all over Holland for his new five-piece band, and by the spring he had his line-up. There was Maurits von Kleef on drums, Dick von Heuvel on the vibraphone, Lex von Weuren on piano and Jac de Vries on bass and saxophone. After several months of rehearsals, Louis Bannet's Rhythm Five made their debut at the Pschoor nightclub in The Hague. 'I even remember the set list from that first night,' Louis recalled years later in Toronto as he rattled off song after song.

'*I Only Have Eyes For You, Heebie Jeebies, After You've Gone, I'm In The Mood For Love, Dinah, Stardust, Blue Moon, Lazy River, Some Of These Days, I Can't Give You Anything But Love, I Got Rhythm, I've Got The World On A String, Bugle Call Rag, Alexander's Ragtime Band, Lullaby Of Broadway, One O'Clock Jump.* The audience was great. For an encore, we came out and played *St. Louis Blues.*' From that night on, it would become Louis Bannet's signature encore song.

Over the next several years, Louis Bannet and his Rhythm Five played all across Holland and central Europe, traveling to Belgium, Germany and Switzerland. Louis also began to sing, winning warm applause for his booming tenor on such numbers as *Blue Moon* and *I Only Have Eyes For You.*

One night in the lobby of a Swiss hotel, a bellboy paged Louis and handed him a telephone. It was the manager of new club called Heck's Café, which was set to open in a few months in Amsterdam. The manager said Mr Heck wanted Louis Bannet and his Rhythm Five to headline on opening night. The following week, the band headed back to Holland to begin rehearsals for the opening.

One evening while on a break from rehearsals, Louis and the band were visited by an old friend, Hein Frank, along with some of his female companions. Louis hadn't seen Hein in several years. Hein said he was following Louis' career and even felt a sense of pride – after all, he was the one who had suggested Louis pick up another instrument. One of Hein's girls requested a song, something by Louis

Armstrong. Louis picked up his horn and led the band in *The Devil And The Deep Blue Sea*. He sang not like Louis Bannet, but like Louis Armstrong. His impersonation was uncanny, and Maurits suggested he try it out in front of a larger audience. So that weekend at a performance at the Pschoor nightclub, Louis repeated his impersonation: the audience went wild. The next day in a review of the show, a newspaper writer praised the performance and crowned Louis 'the Dutch Louis Armstrong'.

Ironically, around this same time, Louis Armstrong himself was embarking on a tour of Europe. He had shows planned for London, Denmark, Paris, and Belgium. The last stop on the tour would be Amsterdam.

Two weeks later in Rotterdam, Leentje Bannet was sitting in her kitchen with her son Isaac. As Isaac leafed through the newspaper, he came across a picture of his brother Louis in an advertisement announcing the grand opening of Heck's Café. He showed it to his mother and suggested that he escort her on opening night and that they keep it a surprise. Leentje Bannet had never seen Louis perform with his band. In fact, the last time she had seen him play was when he performed at Queen Wilhelmina's birthday celebration at the Conservatory. On the night of the Heck's Café opening, she put on the dress she usually wore for Rosh Hashanah. She and Isaac were given a table by the front of the stage. As the lights were dimmed, a spotlight hit the stage and the Rhythm Five took their places. Finally, Louis walked out on to to the stage to a rousing ovation. 'I looked out at the audience and welcomd everyone to the club. I noticed my brother waving to me, and then I saw my mother sitting beside him. I said, "Ladies and gentlemen, I was going to open with an Armstrong song, but I hope you don't mind, my mother is sitting right over there and I'd like to play a song just for her." So I picked up my trumpet and played *My Yiddishe Momma*.'

The next morning, Louis joined his mother and brother for breakfast. Isaac opened the newspaper to a review of last night's show at Heck's and read it aloud. The writer ended his story by saying that 'Louis Bannet, the Dutch Louis Armstrong, has a beautiful future ahead of him.'

Several weeks later, Louis was in his dressing room at Heck's. 'It was the last night of the engagement,' Louis recalled. 'The stage manager knocked on my door. I heard this deep, raspy voice ring out.

12

"So you're the Dutch Louis Armstrong. Well, it's nice to meet you: I'm the American one." It was Armstrong himself. It was fantastic.' They took out their horns and jammed. At one point, Armstrong proudly showed Louis the Jewish Star of David he wore in honor of the Karnovskys, a Russian-Jewish family he worked for as a child in New Orleans, who provided the funds for his first cornet.

The Dutch Louis Armstrong would soon be wearing a Star of David of his own, although it certainly couldn't be called an honor.

4. It Could Never Happen Here

On 8 November 1938, Louis Bannet's career was in full swing, as was Adolf Hitler's. On that terrible day, Nazi hatred against the Jews of Germany erupted in a wave of anti-Semitic violence, the event we now know as *Kristallnacht*. That night, Louis Bannet and his Rhythm Five were in the middle of a three-week engagement at the Lido, one of Amsterdam's hottest nightclubs.

Anti-Semitism was by no means unknown in Dutch society, but in pre-war Holland Jews enjoyed an acceptance and tolerance matched by few countries in the world. This led to a sentiment among the Jews of Holland that what had happened in Germany could never happen in their homeland. Even after Germany invaded Poland in September 1939, most Dutch people were convinced that Holland would remain neutral. They even believed Hitler's reassurances that Germany would honor Dutch neutrality – which made the events of 10 May 1940 all the more shocking.

Louis Bannet and his band were playing in the North Sea resort town of Scheveningen. Louis recalled that eventful day. 'Halfway into the show, I was handed a note by the club's owner and was asked to read it to the audience. The note said that the Germans had invaded Holland. I was in shock. The people in the audience were stunned, many were crying.'

For five days the Dutch fought hard and bravely, but they were no match for the German war machine. On the fifth day, the Germans bombed Louis' beloved city of Rotterdam. When it was over, nine hundred people had been killed, many of whom were children who had been trapped within their schoolrooms as the bombs started falling. In addition, more than 78,000 people were homeless, including Leentje Bannet, her husband, and her son Isaac. The next day, Holland surrendered and life under the Nazis began.

Queen Wilhelmina, for whom Louis had performed so long ago, fled to England with members of the ruling Dutch government and formed a government-in-exile. Her immediate family went to Canada. While in London, the queen spoke weekly to the Dutch people, inspiring them to take heart and to fight against those who would enslave their country. Her speeches served to galvanize the population, and earned her the undying love of the nation.

Louis immediately returned to Rotterdam, but his home and his family's home in the Helmerstraat were in ruins. His friend Pieter Dolk was able to locate him and told Louis that his family was living in a Red Cross shelter. 'Pieter let me borrow his bicycle and I rode through the bombed-out city,' Louis recalled somberly. 'At the shelter there were hundreds and hundreds of people. They were all in shock. They had lost everything. I found my mother and my brother Isaac. My father was in terrible shape. He kept repeating over and over how he had no suit and no watch. The next day, we all moved into my uncle's house. That morning I bought my father a new suit and a watch.

Within a week of the occupation, the Germans said they would not impose their ideology on the Dutch people. This of course served to soothe the population, and even heartened the Jews. But of course it was all a ruse, for Hitler had chosen one his most fanatical followers – a fellow Austrian, Arthur Seyss-Inquart – to run the occupation.

In July 1940, the Germans began issuing the first in a long series of anti-Jewish decrees. At first, many of these early proclamations seemed harmless. But in September the Germans began issuing decrees aimed at destroying Jewish life in Holland, especially life for Jewish entertainers and musicians. 'I remember going to a rehearsal at Heck's. Maurits was the only one there. I asked him where the rest of the band were. He said they were trying to leave the country. He said that we all should leave and took out a piece of paper with all the new laws for Jews.' Decree 127 said all Jews must register themselves. Decree 131 said all Jews must have the letter 'J' stamped on their ID cards. Decree 128 stated that all Jews were barred from riding in cars. Decree 121 forbade Jews from having intercourse with non-Jews. But the decree that affected Louis the most was the Proclamation on the Movement of Jews, which barred Jews from entering concert halls, restaurants or nightclubs. Louis Bannet's life as a musician was over.

It soon became evident that the initial promises the Germans had

15

given the Dutch people were going to be broken in pieces. The Nazis were not going to respect Dutch law, and were intent on imposing their ideology upon the country. Step by step, decree by decree, the Germans were transforming Holland into a totalitarian state. The Dutch Parliament was abolished, as were virtually all of the nation's elected bodies. In the courts, Dutch justice was replaced by German justice, which is to say, no justice. Labor unions lost all independence and were put under the control of the state. In the schools German became the major foreign language children could study. New courses began to be taught, ones, that promoted Nazi racial theories. History textbooks were rewritten, reflecting Nazi thought and deleting any mention of the country's beloved Queen Wilhelmina. In addition, laws were passed prohibiting the displaying of the queen's portrait, and throughout Holland the Germans changed the name of any street that bore her name or any living member of her family.

In February 1942 thousands of mimeographed leaflets were distributed to Dutch workers calling on them to go on a one-day strike in protest against the German mistreatment of the Jews. The strike was organized by the banned Dutch Communist Party. The organizers particularly wanted the participation of the city's municipal workers, especially Amsterdam's streetcar conductors and drivers. The absence of streetcars, the organizers thought, would be very dramatic symbol. The strike was set for 25 February, a Tuesday. Initially there was some hesitation among the streetcar employees, but on the day of the strike, many streetcars never left their depots, and those that did quickly returned. By noon, not a single streetcar was running in Amsterdam. The strike soon spread among white- and blue-collar workers. It took the Germans totally by surprise: nothing like this had happened in any of the cities of occupied Europe. Seyss-Inquart, who was away in Vienna, had left his commissioner for public security, the brutal Hans Rauter, in charge. He ordered troops to be moved into the city and imposed a curfew, which was generally obeyed. In spite of the stringent German censorship, news of the strike spread to other parts of Holland and people in cities such as Haarlem and Zandaam began strikes of their own. By Wednesday, many private sector employees joined the strike. As the day wore on, heavily armed German police and SS officers swarmed through the streets of Amsterdam and other Dutch cities. Many of the instigators were hunted down and arrested. Most would end up in concentration camps. In the face of this insurmountable might, the strike was called off. The February strike was an active repudiation of German occupation. Yes, it was a failure, but a noble one. It had no effect in stopping the Germans or their anti-Semitic policies, but it did confirm that the Germans were not winning, nor would they ever win, the hearts and souls of the Dutch people.

On 29 April 1942, the Germans issued a decree that made it mandatory for all Jews to wear yellow stars. In all, 569,355 cloth badges bearing the word 'Jood' were made. A letter was sent to all Jewish households informing families where the stars could be purchased. The badges had to be sewn on to the clothes – they could not be pinned.

Pieter Dolk, who was a Gentile as well as Louis' good friend, was a member of the underground. He also worked for the underground newspaper, *De Vonk*. To show sympathy for the Dutch Jews, the newspaper printed 300,000 paper stars with the inscription 'Jews and non-Jews are one'. The protest was a failure, and many of those caught wearing the paper stars were arrested.

In May, troubling rumors began circulating within the Jewish community and the Dutch underground that the Germans would soon start deporting Jews to do labor service in Germany. On 26 June 1942, notices went out by special delivery to 4,000 Dutch Jews to report for service. The orders emanated from the Central Office for Jewish Immigration, a bureau set up by a young and eager statistician named Adolf Eichmann. Louis Bannet received a notice, as did Maurits von Kleef. Also notified was Anne Frank's older sister, Margot. For months the Franks had been making preparations to go into hiding, which they thought would happen in July, but on receiving Margot's summons they went into hiding the very next day. The Franks were an exception, for they had a plan. Fortunately for Louis Bannet, he had Pieter Dolk. Pieter thought that Louis Bannet was too well known to hide in a big city such as Amsterdam or The Hague, so he somehow obtained a set of false identity papers and brought his friend to a safe house in a small farming village in the Dutch countryside. Louis Bannet, the Dutch Louis Armstrong, was now Jan Engels.

5. Hidden

As many as 30,000 of Holland's Jews chose to hide, to *Onderduiken*, to submerge, as the Dutch caled it. The case of Anne Frank and her family was somewhat unusual. Most Jews who went into hiding did so alone, like Louis Bannet.

In the summer of 1942, Pieter Dolk brought Louis Bannet, now Jan Engels, to the southern Dutch town of Zwijndrecht. Pieter and Louis's nephew, Louis von Weren, were the only two people who knew of his whereabouts. Louis' new home was a one-room apartment on the second floor of an old brick house. Pieter unlocked the door and Louis followed him into the apartment. Pieter immediately walked over to the windows, closed the shades and drew the curtains.

'You must keep these curtains closed at all times, day and night,' Pieter told Louis. 'You don't know who your neighbors are.'

'You mean I can never go out?' Louis asked.

'If you go out, it must be only at night, and just for a short time,' Pieter instructed. 'As for food, you have enough here for two weeks. I will bring you more when you need it. Do you understand?'

Louis did not answer his young friend.

'Louis, do you understand?' Pieter asked, even more emphatically.

'My name is not Louis, it is Jan Engels,' he answered.

The hiding of Jews in Holland was not a capital offense as it was in countries such as Poland, but Dutch Christians who did hide Jews were threatened with a trip to the Mauthausen concentration camp. Close friendships in wartime Holland between Jews and Gentiles were not that common. This was not necessarily a result of anti-Semitism, but the consequences of what the Dutch called *Verzuiling*. Roughly translated it means 'you stick with your kind and I'll stick with mine'. This may have preserved some social harmony, but it would have dreadful repercussions, because it contributed to the indifference many Dutch Gentiles felt toward the Jews and their plight. Of the 30,000 Jews who went into hiding, more than half were caught, turned in by their fellow countrymen.

In late October of 1942, Pieter Dolk drove up from Amsterdam to bring Louis some supplies, as well as news about his family and the war. As he approached the house, he noticed two Dutch Gestapo agents talking to a woman who lived across the street. He circled the house several times until they were gone. He parked his car in the back and went up the stairs to Louis's apartment. He gave three short knocks on the door, followed by three longer ones. Louis opened the door and took some of Pieter's bags.

'Louis, it's not safe here any more,' Pieter said nervously. 'I saw two Gestapo men talking to a woman across the street. Has anyone seen you come or go?'

'I've done what you told me. I only go out at night,' Louis said. 'I haven't spoken to anyone or seen anyone.'

'This woman could have seen you from her window. She may have become suspicious, seeing a man who leaves only at night,' Pieter said.

'Pieter, I've been very careful,' Louis said.

'We need to be more careful. Tomorrow you leave,' Pieter said.

The next night, Pieter took Louis to the small farming village of Drimmelen. Pieter found a safe haven in the home of the local baker. His name was von Essel, and he lived next to his shop with his wife and ten children. Somehow, they found room for Louis. Pieter also arranged for Louis to work during the day. He found him work as a bookkeeper for a man named von Hurvel, who ran the village water-mill. Each day, Louis would leave his small room at the baker's home and walk through the village to his job at the watermill. Of course, in a city such as Amsterdam or The Hague, people would have instantly recognized the Dutch Louis Armstrong. But Drimmelen was a village made up mostly of farmers, and they rarely ventured into the big city.

At night, Louis would sit alone in his room and listen to the radio Pieter Dolk had left for him. One evening he heard a broadcast from the BBC in London about how the Germans were sending Jews to camps in Poland, where they were killing them by the thousands. He thought the story was so far-fetched that he turned the dial in search of some music.

In the days ahead, Louis tried to blend into village life as much as possible, even attending church on Sunday.

But soon his fame would betray him.

The woman who helped Pieter find a safe house for Louis in Drimmelen also happened to be a friend of Louis' nephew. She was a Gentile, and a big fan, so Louis' nephew gave her a poster of Louis. It was a poster similar to the posters displayed in front of the night-clubs of Amsterdam, with Louis holding his trumpet, hair slicked back, standing proud, dressed in his trademark gray tuxedo.

One morning in mid-December, two Dutch Gestapo agents paid her a visit. Whether she had aroused suspicion or had been informed on by someone in the village no one was ever sure. The two agents began to interrogate her about her role in finding safe houses for Jews. One of the men spotted the poster of Louis Bannet, walked over to where the poster was hanging and tore it off the wall.

'Where is this man?' the Gestapo agent asked.

'I don't know,' she replied.

'We think you do know,' the other agent said.

For the next hour they beat and tortured her, until she finally revealed where Louis Bannet could be found.

Several streets away, Louis was sitting in the baker's shop. 'I was sipping a cup of tea and reading the newspaper,' Louis remembered. 'The date on the front page was 15 December 1942. I even remembered what I was reading. It was a story about the leader of the Dutch Nazi Party, Anton Mussert.' How ironic that two of his most ardent disciples should just now enter the shop. Louis didn't look up from his newspaper as the two Gestapo agents entered the bakery and walked towards his table.

'"This is a nice picture, Louis Bannet,' one of the agents said.

'I instantly knew I had been found out,' Louis recalled, 'but I tried to remain still, keeping my eyes on the newspaper.'

'Are you deaf?' the agent said, raising his voice.

'I said this is a nice picture, Louis Bannet,' he repeated, as he pulled the poster from under his coat.

'My name is Jan Engels, I don't know what you're talking about. Here are my ID papers.'

'*This* is your ID paper!' the agent said emphatically, holding the poster in front of Louis' face. Then he said something Louis could never forget. 'He said he and his wife used to come to all of my shows in Amsterdam. I never thought I would be arrested by a fan.' The other agent lifted Louis up by the arm, turned him around, and began to place handcuffs on his wrists.

'Is this necessary? Can't you just let me keep my hands in my pockets? Where am I going to run to?' Louis asked.

Louis' request fell on deaf ears, and he was led away from the bakery.

At the time of his arrest, Louis had in his possession 42,000 guilders, some gold, his priceless Hungarian violin and his trumpet. All were confiscated and sent back to the Fatherland. All that Louis was allowed to keep was a suitcase with some clothes and his gray tuxedo.

He was taken to the town hall in Drimmelen and placed in a jail cell in the basement. Later that day, as he sat alone in his cell, he heard a knock on the door.

'Who's there?' Louis asked.

'I can't tell you who I am, but I know why you are here. Is there anything I can do for you?' the voice asked from behind the door.

'You can let me out,' Louis answered.

'That I cannot do. Is there someone I can get a message to?' the voice asked.

'Yes,' Louis said. 'Tell von Essel the baker that Jan Engels is dead.'

To the day he died, Louis never knew whom the voice at the door belonged to.

Two days later, Louis was taken to German Gestapo headquarters in Rotterdam for interrogation. He was brought to an office furnished with just a desk and two chairs. He was seated, and was left alone. 'I noticed a strange object on the desk,' Louis said as he recalled this frightening encounter. 'It was the tail of a cow, dried and hard. A Gestapo officer entered the room and sat behind the desk. He signed some papers, filed them away in a draw, and picked up the cow's tail in his hand. He walked behind me and began to ask me questions.'

'I'm not interested how you were hidden, Louis Bannet. I simply want to know who gave you your false ID papers.'

'I bought them from a man on the street in Rotterdam,' Louis answered.

'What was his name?' the officer asked.

'I don't know his name, he was a stranger who just came up to me,' Louis answered.

Louis felt a sharp crack as the sting of the whip ripped the back of his head.

'Tell me who gave you your papers,' the officer demanded as he swung the whip again at Louis' head.

'I'm telling you I don't know who it was,' Louis cried as he tried to block the barrage of blows.

The officer, feeling Louis was not going to divulge any names, called for a soldier and had Louis taken away.

Louis was taken to Amsterdam, to the so-called Joodse Schouwburg, the Jewish Theater. Before the war it had been one of the city's most glittering theaters, with a stage Louis knew well. Now the Nazis used it as a detention hall for Jews. Louis remained there a few days, filling out endless forms. Then he was placed in a special streetcar and taken to the Central Station. There he boarded a sealed train, which took him, and thousands of others, to Westerbork, cynically named the 'Jerusalem of the Netherlands'.

The camp of Westerbork was situated about fifteen kilometers from the village of Westerbork. The camp had been opened by the Dutch authorities during the summer of 1939 in order to receive Jewish refugees arriving from Germany. The first refugees arrived in Westerbork on 9 October 1939. When the German army invaded Holland, there were 750 refugees in the camp. On 1 July 1942, the German authorities took control of Westerbork and it became officially a 'transit camp'. But transit to where? That question was answered two weeks later, when the first transport left Westerbork for 'an unknown destination in the east'.

'I remained in Westerbork for two weeks,' Louis said. 'On Monday evening, 21 January 1943, I was told that I would be leaving the next morning. I rose the next day and took my tuxedo from my suitcase. I put on the gray waistcoat and trousers, draped an overcoat around my shoulders and walked to the train.'

6. Play for your Life

Of the 516 people who left the Westerbork Deportation Camp on 22 January 1943, Louis Bannet was surely the only one wearing a tuxedo jacket under his coat. Inside the packed windowless cattle car, he positioned himself near a small crack in the wall where he could see the landscapes change. The chugging of the train, the chattering teeth, the moans of the old men and women, the cries of the babies, all seemed to blend together into a mournful rhythm section. At times, the smell of feces and urine forced him to wedge his nose into the tiny crevice in the wall and breathe in the frigid air.

But there was no escape from the feeling of helplessness. Louis Bannet knew he was not headed to perform labor service in Germany, although there had been a time when that might have had the ring of plausibility. It was common knowledge that the labor market in Germany was extremely tight, and that there weren't enough workers to build all the armaments the Nazis needed for their war machine. Jews were needed to work. It had seemed so logical.

Louis curled himself into a corner of the train car. As the hours passed like weeks, the moans and cries began to grow silent. The children, weak, terrified, and frozen, did not stir.

'Across the car I noticed an old man lying on the floor clutching a violin case to his chest,' Louis remembers. 'I crawled across the car, but when I reached the man he was dead. I prised the violin case from his arm and placed it on my knee.' Louis moved his hands over the curves of the weathered leather case and opened the clasps. Even through the stench, he could smell the wood and the rosin. He extended his finger and ran it down the course of the bow, then gently plucked each string. No one turned to see where the sound was coming from. Louis lowered the top of the case, fastened the clasps and sealed it like a coffin.

The train began to slow down and an eerie uneasiness settled in. Some people tried to gather their possessions. In a corner, a group of men faced the wall and prayed. Louis looked through the crack in the wall but he couldn't recognize anything – it didn't resemble any town or village he had seen along the way. Finally the train came to a full stop. Louis thought he heard a drum roll. Then, like a curtain on a stage, the doors were pulled open and white-hot lights flooded the car. The vicious barking of the German shepherd dogs were the first sounds Louis heard in Birkenau, followed closely by the vicious barking of German soldiers.

'Aus! Aus! Schnell! Schnell!' (Out! Out! Fast! Fast!) the voices screamed.

The soldiers began pulling people from the train and onto the ramp. One of the dogs kept jumping up and down, as if it was on a trampoline, its growling face popping up into the opening of the train car. Children screamed in terror as the soldiers holding the dogs laughed. Louis walked to the opening of the car and jumped onto the ramp. 'That's when I saw the man who looked like Clark Gable,' Louis remembers. Perhaps it was his dark mustache and chiseled face, or his uniform, so crisp and tailored, with the German Iron Cross affixed to his chest. Or was it the way he waved his riding crop left and right as if he was conducting a symphony? Louis didn't know he was looking at the Angel of Death, Dr Josef Mengele, just as Mengele didn't know he was looking at the Dutch Louis Armstrong as he gave Louis Bannet a quick glance and directed him to proceed one way. He did the same for 17 other men and two women from the transport. The other men, women and children were directed to go in the other direction – straight to the gas chambers.

Louis and the other men were marched to an open area in the camp a few yards from the main watchtower. They were ordered to form a line and stand to attention. The wind was gusting and snow was beginning to fall. The guards walked down the line of men and counted each prisoner, and then walked back in the direction of the train ramp.

'I'm so cold,' a young man standing next to Louis moaned. He was wearing only a light shirt over his tall thin body. 'I gave my coat and hat to my sister on the train. It was a big brown woolen coat with a fur collar. We wrapped it around each other to keep warm. When they pulled her off, they grabbed her by her collar. She screamed my name and then she was led away.'

'Take my coat,' Louis said, as he removed his gray overcoat. My name is Louis Bannet. I am from Rotterdam.'

'Thank you, my name is Pieter. My family is from Amsterdam.'

'Why are you wearing a tuxedo?' a voice on the other side of Louis asked. 'Did you think this was a formal concentration camp?'

'This is all I had when I was arrested. I am a musician,' Louis said.

'And soon you will be a dead musician, and I will be a dead carpenter,' said the man in a hopeless whisper.

As the first gray light of day appeared, there were just three men standing. During the night, Louis heard the bodies of the other men crumple onto the icy mud. Young Pieter from Amsterdam lay on the ground beside him. Louis bent down, removed his coat and shut his frozen eyelids. The carpenter's prophecy was correct, for he too was dead. His body lay half covered in snow, so that it looked as though he was wrapped in a white blanket. The two men still alive were both on their knees with their heads bowed. Louis couldn't understand why he was still standing. He thought of all the nights he had stood on stage playing his trumpet into the early morning hours. Was this what he had been in training for? He tried to put his hands inside his coat pockets, but they were frozen like claws and he couldn't fit them into the slits of cloth. His lips were sealed shut and he had no feeling in his toes. He saw the wind blowing the drifting snow, but he could barely hear its howl with his ears black from frostbite. Two German soldiers approached the line. Louis explained what happened next.

'They walked up to this man kneeling down at the end of the line, one of the soldiers kicked him in the back and he fell into the snow, which woke him, and he immediately stood up. The other man in the middle of the line began to rise very slowly. They came up to me and one of the soldiers, who was no more than nineteen, told me to take off my coat. He placed it over the shoulders of the other soldier. The soldiers marched us through the mud and snow to a red brick building. Even with my frostbitten ear, I could hear screams coming from inside the building. I thought for a moment about running, but to where? The soldiers opened the door and we walked inside. I saw a group of naked men trying to shield themselves from a heavy stream of water that was coming from a thick black rubber hose. They screamed as the water hit their bodies. The two soldiers ordered us to take our clothes off. I removed my shoes and pants and my shirt. I took off my tuxedo jacket and threw it on the pile of clothes. A soldier rushed up to me and pushed me with the other men against the wall. The hose was turned on and I was hit with a stream of cold water. I yelled in agony as the water hit my frozen ear and I fell to the ground.' A soldier started to shut off the water until it turned into an icy trickle. A prisoner wearing a blue-striped uniform walked into the room, carrying a large pile of prison uniforms under his arms. He walked to where the soldiers were standing and dropped them on the floor. He ran out of the door, but quickly returned pushing a wooden cart. The soldiers ordered each man to grab a uniform and a pair of shoes from the cart. 'When I saw the shoes in the cart, I almost laughed. They were wooden shoes. So this was why the Germans invaded Holland, for the shoes.'

The new prisoners, freshly disinfected, then had their heads shaved. Afterwards they were brought to one of the barracks, where they waited to be tattooed with the numbers that would replace their names. Louis shuffled up to the head of the table where a prisoner held a heavy metal pen. On the table were other pens and glass jars filled with blue ink.

'Roll up your left sleeve,' the prisoner said, speaking in Dutch.

Louis stuck out his arm and spoke back to the prisoner in Dutch.

'How could you do this to another Dutchman?' Louis asked.

The prisoner raised his head to look at Louis.

'If it was up to the Germans, I wouldn't use a pen.'

The prisoner slowly put the pen down and stared closely at Louis.

'I know you. You're Louis Bannet, the trumpet player. Don't you recognize me, Louis? It's me, Hein Frank.'

'Oh my God, Hein Frank,' Louis said in disbelief. 'What are you doing here? Did the Nazis arrest all the pimps in Holland too?'

'Only the Jewish ones,' Hein Frank replied. He pushed his face even closer.

'Listen to me, Louis. There is an orchestra here in the camp. I can help get you in.'

Louis shook his head and looked at Hein Frank as if he were mad.

'What are you talking about? How could there be an orchestra here, there is only mud and dead people,' he said.

Just then, one of the guards, noticing the line wasn't moving, marched up to Hein Frank and told him to hurry.

'Give me your arm,' Hein Frank demanded. He picked up the metal pen and began to write on the upper part of Louis's left forearm.

'Nine, three, six, two, six,' Hein Frank spoke the numbers under his breath. He then lifted his head slightly and said, 'I will come for you, 93626.'

The average life expectancy at Auschwitz-Birkenau for able-bodied men was approximately three to six weeks. Hein Frank was way past his prime. He had arrived on a transport from Westerbork along with 509 men and boys and 477 women and girls on 8 August 1942. After the selection, 315 men and 149 women were spared. Also on that transport was a Carmelite nun, Sister Theresia Benedicta of the Cross, born Edith Stein. She refused to deny her Jewish heritage, and was sent to the gas chamber still dressed in the clothing of her order. She was eventually canonized and made a saint. Hein Frank was certainly no saint, but he was a very good hustler, and by bribing a few guards he was able to secure a position in a section of the camp known as Canada. Canada was where all the personal belongings from all the transports were warehoused. The prisoners called it Canada because, like its namesake, it was a place of riches and abundance. The prisoners who worked in Canada were called Commando Canada and a job in this work detail was considered to be a good one, since there was a chance to obtain food, clothing, and other valuables. One item that there was more than an abundance of was musical instruments. Now Hein Frank didn't know a B flat from an F sharp, but he had worked his trade at some of the best nightclubs in Amsterdam, musicians were some of his best customers, and he knew the difference between a clarinet and a slide trombone, which were all the qualifications he needed to became the instrument pimp for the Auschwitz-Birkenau orchestra. The instruments were stored in a converted horse barn known as the *Musikstube*, or music room. And that is where Hein Frank took Louis Bannet to audition for his life.

The sight that awaited Louis Bannet as he entered the *Musikstube* staggered him. On one wall, separated by a wooden partition, hung an assortment of brass and woodwind instruments, each one polished to a near-blinding shine. Louis had to shield his eyes, as if he had been in a cave for days and was seeing the sun for the first time. On another wall hung the string section – violins, violas, and cellos. Leaning against a table scattered with sheet music was a massive double bass. Nearby were a set of drums and several accordions.

As Hein Frank led Louis in, two other prisoners were standing in a corner, their faces chapped and raw from the cold, their hands black and blue from frostbite.

Louis recognized these men. They were Dutch musicians. Jan de Leve was a saxophone player who had played in a big band led by the pianist Wim Poponek. Herman Pons had played the trombone in the house band at Pschoor's. Lying on a tattered red velvet couch just a few feet away, stabbing at a plate of sausages and potatoes, was Franz Kopka, the capo of the orchestra. Kopka, a Ukranian, was a criminal who had been sent to Auschwitz-Birkenau in 1941. He was a murderer, a thief, and a terrible drummer who had a deep and virulent hatred for Jews and musicians more talented than himself. But in order to keep in favor with the SS officers and the camp commander, who thought of the orchestra as his private symphony, he knew he had to stock the orchestra with the best musicians he could find. So each member had to audition, whether he was the first violinist of the Warsaw Philharmonic or the Dutch Louis Armstrong.

'So, Frank, you think these filthy Dutch kikes are good enough for my orchestra? Kopka bellowed. 'We will see.'

Hein Frank took a few steps towards Jan de Leve.

'What is your instrument?' Hein Frank asked.

'I play the saxophone,' he replied weakly.

Hein Frank went behind the partition and took down a saxophone from the wall. He walked back and handed it to Jan de Leve, who could barely hold the instrument. He tried to loosen his fingers by pressing down on the valves, but he had no sensation in his hand. He brought the mouthpiece to his cracked lips and blew, but he could manage only a few sour notes.

'Is this what the Dutch call music?' asked Kopka, wiping his mouth with his sleeve. 'Maybe a trip to the showers would help. Do you have another Jew for me, Hollander?' he called out, using the derogatory term the Germans favored.

Hein Frank then asked Herman Pons to choose an instrument. Pons pointed to a trombone hanging on a bottom rung, and Hein Frank went over to retrieve it. Louis Bannet's lips and hands were as frozen as those of his countrymen. 'I noticed a small cast-iron stove in a corner and quietly inched my way towards it,' Louis clearly remembered. Hein Frank gave Pons the trombone. Pons was a tall man, and, despite his frozen hands, he handled the trombone easily. He pulled the slide in and out and brought the mouthpiece to his lips. He breathed in and blew out, but could not get a sound. Meanwhile, Louis placed both of his hands on top of the hot stove. At first he didn't feel the burning heat, but he soon shut his eyes and buried his mouth in the corner of his shoulder to muffle the sound of his pain.

He removed his hands from the top of the stove and began to rub his lips. Pons made another attempt, but his lips were too cracked and stiff to wrap around the mouthpiece. He blew once again but could not make a sound.

'Is there no Jew who can play in my orchestra?' Kopka screamed as Herman Pons was led away. 'I made one last fist with my hand and rubbed my lips,' Louis said. 'As I moved my hand back and forth, blood trickled out between the cracks of my lips.'

Kopka slowly stood up and put his empty plate on the table.

'So far, Frank, we have two for the ovens and none for the orchestra,' he lamented.

Hein Frank quickly ran around the partition and reached for a trumpet. It was a large B-flat rotary valve trumpet. 'There's one more man here,' Hein Frank said as he rushed towards Louis with the trumpet. 'Hein Frank placed the trumpet in my hands and squeezed tight. 'He looked into my eyes and pleaded ... he said, "Louis, you must play for your life."' Louis fingered the valves of the trumpet and raised it to his lips. He gathered his breath and blew into the mouthpiece, but managed only a faint sound. He tried again, but only a few off-key notes sputtered out. A guard began to walk towards him. Louis raised the horn one more time. The first two D notes raised Kopka from his seat. Then came a B flat, followed by another D. When Louis hit two more B flats and moved up to a C, the guard stepped back. As Louis continued with the opening passage to *St. Louis Blues*, Kopka began to edge himself closer to where Louis was standing, seething with jealousy. As Louis strained to reach the final high C, Hein Frank thought of all the times he had heard Louis hit that high note in Amsterdam, and how the crowds went crazy as each note climbed higher and higher. After Louis finished playing, Kopka mockingly clapped his hands together several times. 'It looks like the orchestra has a new trumpet player – this man plays like a cannon,' Kopka said to Hein Frank. Kopka walked up to Louis. 'Tell me, Hollander, do you read music?' he asked.

'Yes,' Louis answered.

Kopka grabbed a piece of sheet music from a table and held it up.

'Let's see if you can play this,' he said. It was the German march *Alte Kammeraden*. Louis lifted the trumpet to his lips and played the rousing tune note for note.

'You have a good ear?' Kopka said.

Louis slowly raised his hand and gently touched his frostbitten ear. 'Only one,' he muttered.

Kopka looked at Hein Frank. 'Take him to the infirmary,' he ordered.

Hein Frank had started to lead Louis out of the *Musikstube* when Kopka called out to him.

'Hollander, you're going to need this.' Kopka picked up the trumpet and handed it to Louis. Louis took the trumpet from the capo and walked out the door with Hein Frank.

Louis Bannet had been in Auschwitz-Birkenau less than twenty-four hours and already he had a gig.

AUTHOR'S NOTE

A few weeks after my story on Louis Bannet appeared in the *New York Times*, I received a letter from Edwina Handy, the great-grand daughter of W. C. Handy, the composer of *St. Louis Blues*. Her remarkable letter began this way.

It is with great pleasure that I am communicating with you. On Tuesday February 13th, 2001 a gentleman who lives in our building walked into our apartment. He held up to his face a newspaper article that read 'The St. Louis Blues Saved His Life At Auschwitz'. Chills ran down my spine, I stood to my feet with tears in my eyes. I know that W. C. Handy's music was often a vehicle of inter-racial goodwill. We know that it was the Louis Armstrongs of the world that globalized the music and presented it and were the interpreters. Little did we know that a song had saved a man's life from the worst horror of the twentieth century.

7. Barrack Five

Unlike Auschwitz, which included twenty-eight brick buildings, Birkenau was the killing center and larger camp. Construction of Birkenau began in October 1941. Erected on swampland, the barracks were partly brick and partly wooden, adapted from horse stables. The musicians of the Birkenau Orchestra lived, if one can use that word, in Barrack Five. The barrack was divided into two sections, with the musicians on one side and the carpenters and craftsmen on the other. Louis called it the *Prominente Lager*, because the carpenters and craftsmen held a prominent place among the SS men, who were often called upon to do valuable building and repair work. One such man whom Louis Bannet remembered quite vividly was a German watchmaker named Heinz Lewin. 'Lewin worked at a large bench in the rear of the barrack,' Louis recollected. 'He was a small, wiry figure, with a watchmaker's glass attached to his eye, and he always seemed to be hunched over his table talking to himself. When I first met him, his table was full of broken watches. I asked him why there were so many. He said these watches all belonged to guards or SS men. I asked him why they were all in pieces. He looked around his workspace, picked up a watch and strapped it to his wrist. He rose up and walked over to a post behind the table. He said,"Let's say for a moment that I am a guard and this post is you. I walk up to the post and say, good morning Jew, have you had your morning smack yet?" He brought his arm back and hit the post hard with his wrist, smashing the watch to bits. He said, "Now you know why I am such a busy man."' Heinz Lewin returned to his table and asked to see Louis' trumpet. He fingered the valves and applied a squirt of lubricant from a can. He then picked up a small hammer and gently banged out some of the dents. He took a long piece of rope from a drawer and looped it through the trumpet.

'Tie this around your waist and never let it leave your side,' Lewin advised.

Years later, Louis described it this way: 'The guards had their guns at their waists, and I had my trumpet.'

The conductor of the Birkenau Orchestra was a Polish violinist named Szyman Laks. By the time Louis arrived in Birkenau at the end of January in 1943, Laks had been in the camp for more than six months, having arrived on a transport from France on 19 July 1942. The transports that brought Jews to Birkenau were filled with some of the finest musicians in Europe. Many came from the great symphony orchestras of Warsaw, Dresden, Paris, and Prague. But most of the Dutch musicians were jazz players, who had played in dance bands throughout central Europe. It was Laks' job to mold this diverse group into a cohesive orchestra.

The musicians' barrack was situated near the main gate, where the words *Arbeit Macht Frei*, 'Work makes men free', were inscribed. But if the Nazis believed that work made men free, they also believed that music made them work better, especially if it was a rousing German march.

In a 1989 poll conducted by Norman Smith of Lake Charles, Louisiana, the German march *Alte Kameraden*, Old Comrades, was voted third on the all-time list of the world's most popular marches. In the winter of 1943, it was number one with the Birkenau Orchestra.

Louis Bannet's first day as trumpet player with the orchestra began around 4.30. Kopka entered the barrack, banging on a frying-pan with a pair of drumsticks.

'Raus, raus!' he yelled, as he stood by the door.

The members of the orchestra rose from their cramped beds of boards and grabbed their instruments. Louis followed the other musicians to a communal bowl, where each man slapped some brown water on his face. They walked out into the cold darkness and marched towards the gate. The fog rose up from the ground, and all Louis heard was the sound of feet dragging through the snow and mud. A few yards away he saw a light moving in little bursts from one spot to another. As he got closer, he saw chairs and music stands assembled in a circular fashion. A young boy, no more than 16, was placing music papers on the stand. He carried a small torch, which he used to open the music to its proper page. Kopka was standing on the podium, waving his arms like a mad conductor. He spotted Louis approaching, and told him to sit near the center of the orchestra. As he took his seat, the young man with the torch placed sheets of music on Louis' stand and turned the light towards his own face.

'My name is Jonas. This is today's music. It is the same as yesterday's.'

Jonas shone the light on the music so Louis could see. It was *Alte Kammeraden*, the tune he had played at his audition.

'Do you know this piece?' Jonas asked.

'Very well,' Louis replied.

As the fog began to lift, Louis was able to see some of the other members of the orchestra. There were several clarinet players and trumpet players. There were trombonists and two French horn players. Louis heard several violinists tuning up in the rear of the orchestra. An old man sat behind a rag-tag set of drums. Beside him, a tall young man stood holding a pair of cymbals. There were several guards tossing little stones at him. They were playing a strange game of catch, trying to see if the young man could catch the stones with the cymbals. As the gray light of day began to make its appearance, Louis heard the sound of men marching towards the gate. The voices of the guards yelling at the men to stay in formation rang through the camp. Kopka motioned to Szyman Laks to mount the conductor's podium. He silently counted off and the orchestra began to play *Alte Kammeraden* as the bedraggled hordes of men walked by. A few of the men looked over at the orchestra. Louis remembered the look on their faces as one of disgust, as if they were asking, 'How can you play music as I'm being marched off to my death?'

The orchestra continued to play as the last groups from the work detail left the gate. As soon as they were out of sight, Kopka hopped onto the podium and pushed Laks aside.

'You filthy Jews … you call that a performance?' he screamed. 'You're lucky the commandant didn't hear you. He would replace all of you and then you all know where you would be?' 'Trumpet player, come up here,' he barked at Louis. 'Show these Jews how to play the march.' Louis left his chair and stepped up to the podium.

'Now listen to a real musician. Go ahead, trumpet player,' Kopka said. Louis began to play *Alte Kammeraden* as Kopka beamed proudly. 'You hear how powerful the notes are? That's what I want to hear from now on. You must play as if it's your final performance. Because it just might be.' Kopka jumped down from the podium and walked back to his barrack for breakfast. Laks told the musicians to return to their barrack. Young Jonas ran from chair to chair picking up the music. By tomorrow, Louis would know it by heart.

The musicians in the orchestra had other jobs as well, but unlike the thousands of other prisoners who did backbreaking manual labor outside the camp, most stayed within the confines of Birkenau so they could be on call to play for a work detail, an execution, the arrival of a transport, or the entertainment of the officers.

Louis Bannet's job was one of the most unpleasant. Every morning after roll-call, he would gather a handful of men, several shovels and a cart and empty the latrines of excrement. The work detail would then take their cargo to a dumping site and bury it in the mud. As the men trudged from one section of the camp to the next, guards and prisoners alike would turn their backs and hold their noses as Louis and his men passed by. Even the smell of death couldn't suppress the stench.

Barrack Five, with its musicians and craftsmen, was a gathering place for many of the guards and SS men. One of the strangest visitors was a young SS officer named Pery Broad. He had been born in Rio de Janeiro in 1921 to a Brazilian father and a German mother. After having been a member of the *Hitlerjugend*, the Nazi youth organization, and then a volunteer in the SS, he was transferred to Auschwitz in 1942; he was so near-sighted that he had been exempted from serving at the front. In June, he was assigned to the camp Gestapo. With his proficiency in several languages, he quickly rose to the position of *SS Unterscharführer*, attaché of the political section. Pery Broad was a cold and calculating killer. He was also a Nazi fanatic who just happened to be a jazz fanatic.

Several weeks after Louis Bannet's arrival, Pery Broad walked into Barrack Five. As he entered, Kopka sprang up from his seat. He thought Broad was going to approach him, but instead he walked right past him and headed straight to Heinz Lewin's worktable.

'Is it ready?' Broad asked Lewin.

Heinz Lewin knelt below his workbench and pulled out a large leather suitcase. He gently placed it on the table and unsnapped the clasps. Inside, lying on a bed of purple velvet, was a deep-red mother-of-pearl accordion. Pery Broad took the instrument out of its case and placed the straps around his shoulders. He ran his long nimble fingers across the keyboard, playing arpeggios in various keys. Louis and some of the other musicians looked back in the direction of

Lewin's table, shocked not just by what they were seeing, but by what they were hearing. It seemed that Broad was not just an accomplished murderer, but also an accomplished musician. When he stopped playing, he complimented Lewin on his workmanship. He took several packets of cigarettes from his coat and slapped them on Lewin's table.

'This should be enough,' he said to Lewin.

Pery Broad then turned around to face the barrack.

'Does anyone know *Tiger Rag*?' he asked, looking at the ragged group of musicians.

His question was met with stoney silence. Louis looked at the man crouching beside him, a Dutch clarinet player named Goldstein. They both seemed confused and puzzled at the question. Broad turned his gaze to Kopka.

'Kapo, do any of your Jews play jazz?' he asked.

'They will play whatever I tell them to,' Kopka answered.

Kopka looked around the barrack and pointed to Louis.

'Hollander, come here and bring your trumpet,' he yelled.

Louis got up from his bed. He motioned for Goldstein to come with him, and they walked over to where Broad was standing.

'Do you know *Tiger Rag* in B flat?' Broad asked Louis.

'I know it very well,' Louis replied. Louis looked at Goldstein to see if he knew the tune, and one of the strangest jam sessions in history was set to begin. Broad began to play the Dixieland classic, squeezing the bellows of his instrument in and out, running his fingers up and down the keyboard and bass buttons. Louis, who had once played this song with Coleman Hawkins in Amsterdam, and with his own Rhythm Five, was now playing it with one of the monsters of the Third Reich. Goldstein joined in, playing the dizzying high-note refrains. Louis played the melody behind Broad's frantic fingering, hitting the accents on each bar. The music must have carried through the camp, because a number of SS men and guards entered the barrack. Kopka, who thought of Louis as his own, was seething with anger and jealousy over Louis' newfound attention. But as quickly as the jam session began, it ended. Broad just stopped playing. He removed his accordion and left it on the floor. Louis and Goldstein continued to play, but soon stopped, their notes quickly petering out. Broad briskly walked out, taking several guards with him. Heinz Lewin went to pick up the accordion and placed it back in its case. Before they left, several SS men approached Louis and told him they wanted him to come to their barrack and play jazz for them. This, of course, made Kopka even angrier.

In the early 1930s, Nazi Propaganda Minister Josef Goebbels described jazz as 'nigger kike music' and banned it from being played in clubs and on radio. He never said anything, however, about concentration camps such as Auschwitz-Birkenau.

8. Life and Death

Every day Louis Bannet played was another day he would live. It was all so horribly simple. Yet there were many who preferred death, even welcomed it.

In a sad twist of fate, one such man was Leon Bloorman, Louis Bannet's violin teacher from the Jewish Conservatory of Music. Though nearing sixty, he had survived the selection process and made it to the orchestra, where he was reunited with his former pupil. But after just a few days, he simply couldn't go on any more. One night as Louis lay on his bed, his teacher came to him.

'Louis, do you know what they made me do today? They made me play my violin while they hanged a man. He was a Frenchman. Other than being a Jew, I don't know what crime he committed. They pulled him on a cart to the gallows. I had to stand behind him and play *Le Marseillaise*. Can you explain such a thing to me?' asked Leon Bloorman.

'I don't have an answer,' Louis said. 'There are no answers here. Just last week they marched the orchestra to the train ramp. There were chairs set up and the music was already on the music stands. It was a waltz. Kopka was standing on the podium and told us to play. The musicians looked around at each other. Who were we playing for? Young Jonas, the boy who gives us our music, told me. He said we were playing for the people on the trains. He said the wind would carry the music so the people could hear it, and they would think, how bad a place could this be if there was music?'

'Louis, you are stronger than me. I don't think I can go on like this much longer,' the teacher tearfully confessed.

'Try to think of this', Louis said. 'The man they hanged today, the last sound he heard was your beautiful playing.'

Despite Louis' attempt to ease the pain of his former teacher, his mind was made up. A few nights later, Leon Bloorman made a run for the wires. But before he reached the electrified fences, he was gunned down. The next morning, the musicians took their place by the gate. They hurried to their chairs and spread out their music. In the first row, a few seats from Louis, a body sat motionless, tied to the chair. It was Leon Bloorman, and around his neck a sign was hung for all who passed by to see. It read: 'I TRIED TO ESCAPE'.

The *Sonderkommando*, the inmates who had the gruesome task of incinerating the bodies of gas chamber victims, had the highest suicide rate in Auschwitz-Birkenau. The musicians, whose music often accompanied those victims, were second.

In the summer of 1943, Hein Frank brought a new member of the orchestra into Barrack Five. To Louis' astonishment, it was his dear friend and drummer, Maurits von Kleef.

'My God, Maurits,' said Louis, 'I thought you were in Switzerland. What happened?'

Maurits began to tell Louis his story.

'I tried to go. I had my papers and even sent my drums to Geneva. I went to Scheveningen to say goodbye to my parents and my sister. Pieter Dolk told me they were hiding in a farmhouse. I was able to stay there a few days. But one night the Gestapo came, and two days later we were sent to Westerbork.'

'Where is your family now?' Louis asked hesitantly.

'We arrived on the same train. I went one way, they went another,' Maurits said as he began to weep.

'Maurits, you have to be strong,' Louis said. This is going to be the toughest gig we ever played.' The next morning when the musicians assembled, two-fifths of the Rhythm Five were now part of the 42-member Birkenau Orchestra.

It's been said that musicians in the camps lived better than other inmates, that they had better food and clothing. That may have been true for the orchestra in the main camp of Auschwitz, but in Birkenau, the center of murder of the Nazi machine, life for musicians was no better. But for Louis Bannet, that was about to change. Here's how Louis described the strange events that took place one night in March 1943. 'I was sleeping when all of a sudden I was shaken from my bed by a group of SS men. At first I thought I was going to be taken outside and shot. But they told me to get my trumpet. It was wrapped in a cloth and I used it for a pillow. The guard told me to bring Maurits, along with some drums and cymbals, Goldstein the clarinet player, and a violinist named Julius. Then we were led outside to a waiting

1. Louis Bannet, violin virtuoso. Rotterdam, 1925.

2. Anton Swan and the Swantockers. Louis Bannet is on the right, holding trumpet. Amsterdam, 1928.

3. Louis and his Yiddishe Momma, Leenjte Bannet. Rotterdam, 1930.

4. Louis Bannet and his Rhythm Five, Pshoor's Café-Restaurant. Amsterdam, 1934.

5. A man and his horn. Louis Bannet,
Amsterdam, 1946.

6. Students from the Jewish Conservatory of Music performing on the streets of Rotterdam, 1921. Louis Bannet is at center with violin.

7. Louis Bannet, on the left, with the Kentucky Five, an ensemble he formed at the Jewish Conservatory. Rotterdam, 1927.

HEADQUARTERS
THIRD UNITED STATES ARMY
CIC DETACHMENT 970/6
APO 403

15 June 1945

SUBJECT: Identification of CIC Employees

TO: U S Military Police and British FSP

    1. This will certify that LOUIS BANNET, whose signature and picture appear below, has served with CIC Detachment 970/6 since 15 June 1945. He is authorized to perform all duties entrusted to him and to bear arms, concealed or otherwise, at all times. No restrictions of travel or curfew are applicable.

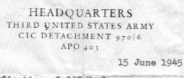

Signature _Louis Bannet._

Clark W. Denton
Special Agent, CIC

8. Louis Bannet's CIC ID papers, issued 15 June 1945 in Bamberg, Germany, authorizing Louis to bear arms, concealed or otherwise, at all times.

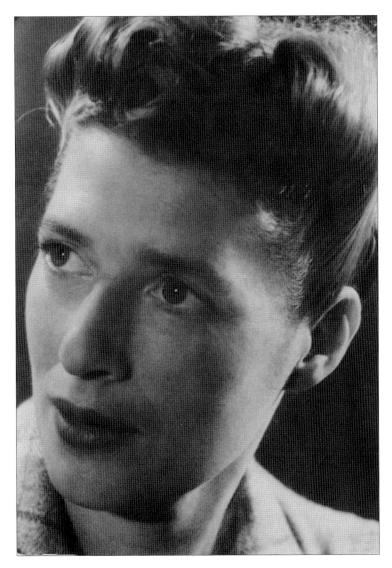

9. His heart was a violin, but it belonged to one woman, Flora.
   The Hague, 1945.

10. The Dutch Louis Armstrong, Montreal, 1956.

11. Louis Bannet, violin student at the Jewish
Conservatory of Music. Rotterdam, 1922.

12. Louis Bannet, as host of the television show *Mon Coeur Est Un Violon*. Montreal, Canada, 1964.

13 Louis and Flora, happy together. Toronto, 2000.

car. The guards loaded the instruments in the trunk, and we all got in the rear of the car. As the car drove away, we noticed Pery Broad sitting in the front seat. He said there was a party for one of the officers, a birthday party, and we would be playing for the guests. I asked Broad what should we play, and he said it should be happy music. 'After all,' he said, 'it's a party.'

The car traveled through the dark wintry Polish countryside. While Pery Broad sat silently in front, Louis tried to compose a set list of songs in his head. He tried to remember a typical set list from the Lido in Amsterdam. He usually opened up with *Stardust* or *Ain't Misbehavin'*. Then a couple of slower numbers such as *I Only Have Eyes For You* and *I'm In The Mood For Love*. Then he would liven things up a bit with *Chicago* and *Tiger Rag*, usually closing, of course with *St. Louis Blues*. Would they make him play *Deutschland Über Alles*?

'As the car began to slow down, I could see a large country house coming into view,' Louis recalled. 'There were many other cars and soldiers parked outside. Broad told the driver to go to the rear of the house. There were several soldiers standing about. The car stopped and the driver hurried out to open the door for Broad. Broad stepped out and asked some of the soldiers to take the instruments from the trunk into the house. He opened the passenger door and told us to come out. I remember the soldiers were quite shocked at the sight of four camp inmates, in their blue and white striped uniforms, coming out of the car. Broad told one of the soldiers to take us to a second-floor parlor. We marched passed the kitchen and I got the first smell of real food in months. We were led up the stairs to a landing overlooking the first floor, where our instruments were waiting. Through the railing, I could see tables laden with food and drink. Maurits quickly set up his drums and three chairs were placed in front of the drums for me, Goldstein, and Julius. Broad came up the stairs and studied the set-up. He told the soldiers to bring up some large plants from downstairs and place them in front of us. He said he wanted us to be heard, not seen. He told us the guests would be arriving shortly, and he'd send someone up to tell us when to begin. I went over some of the songs we would play with Julius and Goldstein. I began to hear the sound of voices and laughter from the room downstairs. A soldier ran up the stairs and told us to begin. I gave a quick look to Maurits, Goldstein, and Julius, and we started playing *Stardust*.'

As the notes of Hoagy Carmichael's classic song echoed through the house, the guest of honor entered the room. It was Dr Mengele's birthday. Louis was able catch a brief glimpse of Mengele as he walked past a small gap in the plants. He had not seen him since that first day on the train ramp, but he had heard stories from other prisoners about his ghastly medical experiments. As Goldstein picked up the melody on clarinet, Louis got a glimpse of some of the other guests. There were many officers, and women dressed in exotic colors. Louis recognized them as Gypsies. There were also several sets of twin boys standing close to Mengele. The quartet finished *Stardust* and then went into *Ain't Misbehavin'*. Some of the officers began dancing with the Gypsy women. As the evening went on, Louis and the other musicians were able to see some of the acts of sexual depravity that were taking place below. Through it all, they continued to play. After nearly two hours, the guests began to disperse. A soldier came up and told the musicians to pack up their instruments. In the parlor behind the landing where they played, Maurits noticed several plates of half-eaten food on a table. He called over to Louis, Goldstein and Julius. They quickly opened their music cases and scraped the plates clean.

On the drive back to the camp, Pery Broad told Louis how much Dr Mengele had enjoyed his music. But all Louis and the musicians could think about was the food hidden in their cases.

The next morning, Louis and the quartet treated some of the members of the orchestra to a breakfast of cold sausage, stale bread and potatoes.

News of Louis and his 'Birkenau Quartet' spread quickly among some of the jazz-loving SS men, and it wasn't long before Szyman Laks was getting daily requests for Louis to come and play evening concerts in their rooms. This arrangement benefited everyone, even the jealous Kopka, since Louis and the other musicians were often paid in the currency of the camp, cigarettes, of which Kopka took more than his share. Occasionally the musicians were given German chocolate, which they tried to keep away from Kopka and share only with the rest of the orchestra.

During some of these evening soirées, Pery Broad would sometimes sit in with his accordion. He must have welcomed these jam sessions, considering how he spent his days, overseeing the murders of tens of thousands in the gas chambers.

One day, Hein Frank was removing luggage and other personal

belongings from a recently arrived transport. A few yards from the ramp, he noticed a man lying on the ground while two SS men stood talking over him. He recognized this man instantly. It was Isaac Bannet, Louis' brother. He had met him many times at the clubs where Louis played. He was able to overhear one the guards mention that this man had gangrene and should be sent to the quarantine barrack. Hein Frank rushed back to Barrack Five, where he found Louis sitting with Maurits.

'Louis, your brother Isaac is in the camp. I just saw him,' Hein Frank said excitedly.

'Isaac? Are you sure?' Louis said in disbelief.

'He was taken to the quarantine barrack. I heard one of the SS men say he had gangrene.'

'If he has gangrene, he can't work. If he can't work, he'll be gassed. I have to get him out,' Louis said.

'The quarantine barrack is in another part of the camp. How can you reach him?' Maurits asked.

'I pass the quarantine barrack everyday on my latrine detail. Hein, do you know any of the doctors in the infirmary?' Louis asked.

'Yes, Dr Onterescu,' Hein answered.

'Tell him to expect a new patient tomorrow,' said Louis.

'The next morning, I gathered the work detail together and told them of my plan,' Louis recalled many years later. As I approached the gate, I called out to the guard, "93626 plus five!" and the guard waved us through. We made our usual stops at the latrines, shoveling the shit into the cart. As we approached another checkpoint, I announced again, 93626 plus five. The guard held his nose, waved us through. Finally we reached the quarantine barrack. I quickly ran inside and saw my brother Isaac lying on a blanket on the floor. I had not seen him since I went into hiding. I bent down and held his hand – he was burning with fever. I said, "Isaac, I have to get you to a doctor, and this was the only way to do it. Some day, I hope you'll forgive me." I lifted him up and brought him outside and gently placed him into the cart filled with the shit of Birkenau and told him to keep his head down. The men picked up their shovels and we began to head back. As we approached the first checkpoint, I called out once more. "93626 plus five!" The guard, shielding his nose from the stench, waved us through. At the final checkpoint, we were again sent on our way, but instead of heading for the dumping hole, I steered the cart to the infirmary. I found Dr Onterescu and left my brother with him. I didn't know if that would be the last time I would see him.'

Years later, Louis told this remarkable tale about this courageous Jewish doctor.

'Camp Commander Schwarzhuber had a young son. One day the boy was playing with his father's pistol when the gun went off and a bullet became lodged in his head. Dr Onterescu's reputation as an accomplished surgeon was well known in the camp, and he was called upon to save the boy's life. Which he did. Several months later, the doctor contracted typhus. When several of the camp's Jewish doctors asked Commander Schwarzhuber for medicine, he refused, and the doctor who had saved his son's life was left to die.'

9. Last Dance of the Gypsies

According to the Race Laws set forth at Nuremberg in 1935, Europe's Gypsies were defined as non-Aryan. In official language, they were deemed parasites and considered unworthy to live.

On 26 September 1942, two hundred Gypsies had been transferred from Buchenwald to Auschwitz and assigned to build the new Gypsy camp, BIIe, at Birkenau. On 26 February 1943, the first transport of Gypsies arrived at the newly erected Gypsy 'family camp'.

The Gypsy camp was approximately two kilometers from Birkenau. It was also the working home of Dr Mengele. Dr Mengele usually got whatever he wanted, and after the success of his birthday party, what he wanted was his own orchestra, an orchestra made up of Gypsies. Mengele gave this assignment to Pery Broad. But this was 1944, the transports were arriving in greater numbers, and Broad's time was consumed by the killings. He turned to Louis Bannet.

One afternoon, Pery Broad came into Barrack Five looking for Louis. Kopka was standing near the door, and Broad pushed him aside.

'Where is the trumpet player?' he demanded.

Kopka quickly went to get Louis and practically dragged him from his bed to the waiting Broad.

'What do you think you're doing?' Broad screamed at Kopka. 'This man is real musician, not a swine like you.' Broad began to repeatedly smack the capo across the face.

'Come with me,' Broad ordered Louis.

Kopka fumed as Louis and Broad walked out of the barrack. The two marched out of the main gate, down a long, muddy road. Louis could only wonder where he was being taken. And why.

Finally they came upon the Gypsy camp. As they walked into the camp, Louis was amazed to see men, women, and children all together, wearing colorful clothes and not uniforms. They entered a barrack where about thirty Gypsy men and a handful of women were waiting. Many of the men were holding violins; some had accordions, mandolins and guitars. Pery Broad stood in the center of the room and called on the crowd for silence.

'This man is a famous musician who plays in the camp orchestra,' Broad announced to the room. 'Dr Mengele would like to have his own orchestra here in this camp. This man will help you put together a fine orchestra. In a few weeks there will be a Sunday concert. I know by that time you will be ready.' Broad finished his remarks, said a few words to Louis, and then left the barrack. The Gypsies eyed Louis with obvious suspicion. Up until that point, they had had little or no contact with anyone other than their own kind. When they were deported in March of 1943 from occupied Europe, they boarded the transports in family units, and that's how they remained. After an awkward few moments, Louis picked up a violin from the table and started to pluck a few strings. He picked up a bow and began to play an old Hungarian melody he knew from his youth. Several of the Gypsy musicians began to play along. A young dark-haired woman began to dance around the room. When the music came to a stop, the young woman introduced herself to Louis.

'My name is Anita,' she said. 'I am the daughter of the barrack elder.'

'I'm Louis Bannet. The SS man said that I must come here each day to rehearse the orchestra. Will you help me get them ready?' Louis asked.

'Why should we play for the people who are going to murder us?' Anita asked Louis.

'I do not play for them,' Louis answered. 'I play for me.'

Louis returned almost every evening to the Gypsy camp for rehearsals. Sometimes Kopka, who was seeing a woman in the camp, would accompany him. Watching Louis conduct the Gypsy Orchestra with Broad looking on fueled Kopka's jealousy.

As the days went by, Anita was becoming infatuated with Louis, and each time she saw him, she professed her love. He tried to explain the futility of such behavior, but she would not listen.

The Sunday of the concert was a warm spring day. As Louis entered the camp, the scene that unfolded before him seemed like a dream. All the camp inhabitants were out of their barracks, dressed in colorful costumes. There were men swinging from rings and high bars. A woman was walking a tightrope that was fastened between two gasoline drums. Many of the older children performed tumbling tricks. Taking all this in, as he stood on the steps of the infirmary, was Dr Mengele. Pery Broad told Louis to begin the concert. Louis motioned for the musicians to come together and join him on a makeshift stage that had been constructed for the occasion. Anita brought him his violin and bow. With his trumpet still fastened to his waist, Louis placed the violin upon his shoulder and began to play the emotional strains of the *Romanian Rhapsody*. As the orchestra joined in, the crowds of Gypsy families swayed and spun in circles to the music. When it was over, Pery Broad congratulated Louis on a job well done. Louis asked him if he would be coming back to the camp tomorrow.

'That won't be necessary,' Broad answered. 'The entire camp is being sent away to another camp.'

Louis understood all too well what that meant. A few moments later, Anita ran to Louis and threw her arms around him. She wept as she spoke of her love for him. Louis removed her arms from around his neck. He noticed a dark mark on her wrist.

'What is this?' he asked.

'I tattooed your name on my arm to show my love,' Anita confessed.

'This is crazy, Anita. You've got to listen to me. The Germans are going to empty this camp. They're going to send everyone to the gas chambers. You have to do something, you have to hide,' Louis said frantically. Just then a piercing whistle ripped through the camp and everyone was ordered to their barrack. Anita's father came and took his daughter and led her to the barrack. Soon after, a convoy of trucks swept through the camp. The SS began to round up the Gypsies, but the prisoners fought back with improvised knives, shovels, sticks, and stones. This skirmish only forestalled the inevitable, of course. By the summer of 1944, the Gypsy camp and most of Europe's Gypsies were gone.

10. From One Hell to Another

Over the next weeks, Kopka's hatred and jealousy of Louis intensified. Whether it was because of Louis' stature among the musicians, or his relationship with Pery Broad, Kopka wanted to put an end to Louis Bannet's career. One morning, he found a way to do it.

When a trumpet player warms up, he blows saliva into his mouthpiece. That was precisely what Louis was doing this chilly morning before roll-call. Unfortunately, just at that moment, Kopka was passing by and was hit with spray from Louis' trumpet.

'You filthy Dutch Jew' Kopka growled. 'How dare you spit at me? I am still the capo of this orchestra and I can throw anyone out, even you, Hollander.' Kopka swiped Louis' trumpet out of his hands. 'When the work detail leaves the gate this morning, you will join them,' the capo ordered.

This was a death sentence for Louis. He was ordered into a work crew with prisoners who had no particular skill. He had seen work crews like this pass before him every day. Usually 100 men would march out and 75 bodies would come back.

That morning, the prisoners marched to a field lined with broken airplane parts; they were from planes returning from the front. The pieces of metal weighed hundreds of pounds and the men had to lift them on to trucks. Many men, skeletons already, collapsed and died. Those who couldn't work were beaten or shot. Though bruised and bloodied, Louis somehow survived the day. As the work crew began its march back to camp, several men fell to the ground, almost begging for death. Soon, Louis could see the main gate and he could hear the orchestra. They were playing *Berliner Air*, a march that was also part of the repertoire on the *Titanic*. Even though his feet felt like bricks, he too began to march in step. What was left of the work detail had just passed the main gate, when a voice ordered them to halt. A soldier walked up to the detail. He was tall and broad-shouldered. Louis knew this guard well, having played for him many times.

Louis called him Carnera, because of his resemblance to the great Italian heavyweight fighter, Primo Carnera. Carnera was shocked when he saw Louis.

'What are you doing here, Louis?' he asked. 'Why aren't you with the orchestra?'

Louis told him about Kopka and what happened during morning roll-call. Carnera was furious, and he told one of the soldiers to bring Kopka to him immediately. He asked another soldier to get some water for Louis. Kopka was brought to Carnera.

'Why did you send this man out of the orchestra?' Carnera demanded to know.

'This filthy Jew spat at me,' Kopka said.

Carnera exploded, inflicting a barrage of slaps and punches on Kopka's face.

'If this happens again,' Carnera warned, 'it will be you who marches out. Now get his trumpet and bring him to his chair.'

After this episode, Kopka seemed to disappear. Some thought he had been sent to the front, while others guessed he had been taken out and shot. Then a few weeks later, Louis found a note on his bed from Kopka. It was an apology and a plea for help. He had developed typhus and was in quarantine. He knew Louis was a friend of one of the doctors, and begged him to ask for medicine. Louis read the note, crumpled the paper and tossed it into the stove.

As it became evident that the war would not end their way, the Germans began gassing and burning bodies at a faster rate. The Polish clerical workers also began to burn records, and with Allied forces moving in, the Germans started moving prisoners out. Louis was sitting with Maurits on their beds when Hein Frank approached them.

'Tomorrow morning they will begin shipping out prisoners. The musicians and carpenters will be among the first to go,' said Hein Frank.

'Go? Go where?' Louis asked.

'To another camp,' Frank answered.

'Why the musicians?' Louis wondered.

'They probably want us to play at Hitler's wedding,' said Maurits.

'What about you, Hein? Will you go too?' asked Louis.

'Someone has to stay and open the gates for the Russians,' he said.

Louis placed his arm on Frank's shoulder.

'You saved my life, Hein Frank,' he solemnly said.

'Louis,' Hein said as he clutched his old friend to his chest, 'you did what you always did, you played for your life.'

* * *

Hein Frank, who implored Louis Bannet to play for his life, wasn't able to extend his own. He died of typhus a few months before Allied forces liberated the camps. SS Officer Pery Broad was captured on 6 May 1945 in the British occupation zone. Because he spoke English so well, he became an interpreter for the British authorities. In 1945 he wrote a long memoir about his experience in Auschwitz, and on 13 July he turned it over to representatives of the Intelligence Service. In his memoir he says nothing whatsoever about his own role, and blames his colleagues for the atrocities. On 29 September 1947, Broad's memoir was translated into English and used at the Nuremberg Trials regarding the gas chambers as mechanisms of mass murder. Later that year, Pery Broad was released. But many years later he was indicted along with other former SS members from Auschwitz and put on trial. The trial took place in Frankfurt-am-Main and lasted from December 1963 to August 1965. During the trial his 1945 memoir, in which he accused several of his co-defendants of atrocities, was presented to Broad. He admitted he was the author, and was surprised, since he had made no mention of his own complicity in the exterminations. He had also made no mention of something Louis Bannet told me: that it was Broad who smuggled sheet music into the camp, music written by Jews such as Irving Berlin, Harold Arlen, and Arthur Schwartz. For his crimes against humanity, Pery Broad was sentenced to four years in prison.

* * *

The next morning, nearly two years after his arrival, Louis Bannet, along with Maurits and many other musicians, left Birkenau for a fate they did not know. Before they boarded the open cattle car, each prisoner was given a chunk of bread. Louis was certain it was poisoned, but he thought he was going to die anyway; at least he'd die with something in his stomach.

The train left Poland and entered Germany. It came to a stop 35 kilometers from Berlin in Sachsenhausen-Oranienburg. A familiar sound greeted the prisoners from Birkenau: barking dogs and their equally vicious guards. The prisoners were taken from the train and brought to a huge airplane hanger filled with thousands of prisoners from other concentration camps. By now, Louis considered himself a professional prisoner. After all, he had two years under his belt, which may not seem like a lot, but in Birkenau it was a lifetime. Louis also knew all the tricks, so he sought out the people he thought could help him most: the doctors. As it turned out, the medical staff in Sachsenhausen were mostly Dutch doctors, many of whom knew Louis from Holland. One was a violin player, and he, Louis, and Maurits gave an impromptu concert in the middle of the hangar to thousands of men starving for food and freedom.

Louis and Maurits stayed in Sachsenhausen for just a few weeks. Then, with hundreds of prisoners, they were put on a train and taken to a sub-camp of Buchenwald, a forced labor camp called Ohrdruf. Upon his arrival, an SS man, spotting Louis' trumpet, told him that there was no orchestra in this camp and he would have to work like any other Jew. Rolf Bauman, a German Jew, who was perhaps the most prominent prisoner in Birkenau because he was in charge of giving out work assignments, was also sent to Ohrdruf, where he was given the same job. He knew Louis well and realized his predicament: without an orchestra, what could he do? But there were no easy jobs in Ohrdruf. The main work of the camp was the building of underground caverns, which the Nazis planned to use to house their headquarters and armaments factories. Prisoners were also used to lay railroad tracks. Bauman assigned Louis to a work detail of carpenters who were doing repair work at a castle that the Nazis hoped would be an officers' retreat. Louis may have been a virtuoso on two instruments, but he had never held a hammer in his life. The soldier in charge of Louis' work detail was an older man who had recently returned from the Eastern front. Louis thought that he must have been wounded, because he walked with a severe limp. He brought Louis to a section of the castle that had been hit by Allied bombing, and he told him to fix a damaged door. Louis looked at the wood and tools that had been left for him. It was like asking someone who never held a violin to play a Beethoven concerto. He tried the best he could to repair the damage, but when the soldier returned to inspect the work, it was obvious Louis was no master craftsman. The soldier

uncanny ability to play the right song at the right time. One of the most popular songs in Germany in the 1930s and 1940s was a sentimental tune called *Heimat deine Sterne*, which means Homeland Your Stars. It was a song about the longing for a peaceful life, loved ones, family, and above all, home. Now keep in mind this was December 1944. The Germans were losing the war. There would be no leave this Christmas for the soldiers of the Third Reich, and home and family would surely be on their minds. Louis knew the melody well, and, even with two strings, he was able to capture its melancholy refrain. The officer stood and listened, then quietly began to sing as tears welled up in his eyes.

> *Homeland, your stars.*
> *They radiate to me from a far place.*
> *The sky is like a diamond.*
> *A thousand stars stand far away.*
> *Sent by the dearest one, friendly me.*
> *In the distance I dream about the homeland.*

'You must play this for my wife,' the officer said, as he reached for the telephone on his desk.

Louis was puzzled. He looked at Jonas, then walked over to the desk. The officer told Louis to place the violin near the receiver, as he dialed the number.

'Hello Liebchen,' he cooed into the phone. 'I have a surprise for you. Just keep listening.'

Louis began to play *Heimat deine Sterne* into the telephone receiver. As he played, several SS men gathered by the doorway to listen. The SS officer again sang along with Louis, bringing his face closer to the phone. When he finished, the SS men waiting at the door came up to Louis and told him that he must now play for their wives and girlfriends. So Louis went from office to office, serenading the mothers and daughters of the Fatherland. He played Christmas songs and lullabies, and someone even managed to find the two missing strings. When a group of soldiers from town came by, they asked him to play for their families too, but Louis told them he was too weak and tired. So the soldiers gave him a meal and a bath, and even let him rest before he resumed his telephone concerts.

Unlike other camps, Ohrdruf had no sophisticated tools of mass murder, but the Germans made up for that in man-made brutality.

Thousands of prisoners were starved, shot or clubbed to death as Allied forces neared the camp. The prisoners who were spared this fate, such as Louis and Maurits, left Ohrdruf on a death march to Buchenwald, nearly eighty kilometers away. It was late February 1945, and the bitter cold and biting winds took the lives of many prisoners.

'The minute you stopped, the guards threatened to shoot,' Louis remembered. 'Some begged to be shot, they were so sick. I still had some food in my stomach, some bread here, some bread there from playing, so I had a little strength.'

Before they reached Buchenwald, Louis remembered marching through the town of Weimar.

'We begged the people in the town for water, but the soldiers yelled at them not to give the Americans any water. The Americans? We were not Americans, we were Jews. But the Americans were coming and the soldiers were trying to trick the people into thinking we were Americans,' he said.

By the winter of 1945, Buchenwald was filled with tens of thousands of prisoners arriving from concentration camps that were being emptied as American and Russian forces approached. Again, fate entered Louis' life in the form of a man named Kosfuring, a Jewish political prisoner from Amsterdam. He lived in a barrack with other political prisoners and regularly received packages from the Red Cross. These men all knew Louis from Holland, and they shared their food with him and Maurits.

But eventually Buchenwald had to be emptied too, and in the spring of 1945 Louis found himself again in an open cattle car bound for an unknown destination. In the confusion of Buchenwald's final days, Louis became separated from Maurits. The train car was packed tight, and many people died during the journey. When someone died, their body was thrown from the train to make more room. Louis wondered if one of those bodies was his friend and drummer. The train came to rest in a small village a few kilometers from Prague. When the doors opened, it was a scene of mass chaos. Men and women in civilian clothes were walking towards the train carrying baskets of bread. Louis again believed they would all be poisoned. Then he noticed the people were wearing Red Cross armbands. He stumbled out of the train, still unsure of what was taking place. He thought he heard someone say the war was over, but he was weak and delirious. He crawled along the ground, dragging his trumpet along with him, when he spotted an old soldier he recognized from Birkenau. The soldier was quickly removing his uniform. Underneath, he was wearing blue and white prison stripes, thinking he could conceal his identity and pass himself off as a Jew. Louis slowly got up and stumbled towards the soldier, picked up a piece of wood from the ground and, with his last ounce of strength, smashed the soldier's skull. It was 6 May 1945, and the war was over. But Louis Bannet wouldn't know that until six weeks later, when he awoke from a coma in a hospital in Prague. Laying in bed in the hospital ward, feeling the soft white sheets on his skin, Louis rose up with a great sense of relief. He was convinced that the last two and a half years of his life had all been a horrible dream. How could it have been real? A beautiful young nurse came to see him. She was holding an old violin.

'We knew you were a musician, because you were carrying your trumpet when they brought you in,' she said. 'We thought you might like to have this violin. No one else here can play it.'

'Thank you,' Louis said. 'Can you tell me how long I've been here?'

'Nearly six weeks, ever since the war ended,' she answered.

When he heard those words he realized his nightmare was not a dream.

'Do you have a mirror?' Louis asked.

The nurse took a small mirror from her pocket and handed it to Louis. He brought the mirror to his face and let out a gasp. He quickly turned his head to look behind him, but no one was there. The face he didn't recognize in the mirror was his own.

11. G I Lou

Beginning at Westerbork in 1942, and ending in Thereisenstadt, where he was sent briefly after his hospital stay in Prague, Louis Bannet had been in six different camps. Now, in June 1945, he entered his last – a displaced persons (DP) camp in Bamberg, Germany. Bamberg was located in Bavaria, not far from Hitler's retreat at Berchtesgaden. It became the temporary home for tens of thousands of Jewish and non-Jewish refugees from all over Western Europe. Bamberg was also home to the First Battalion Army Band, led by Lieutenant James Murphy. One afternoon, Lieutenant Murphy was walking through the camp when he noticed a crowd of people dancing and singing to the sound of a lone trumpet. It was Louis, giving an impromptu concert for a group of Dutch Jewish refugees. He was playing Jewish songs and American standards. For many, it must have been the first time they had smiled or laughed in years. Afterwards, Lieutenant Murphy asked Louis if he would like to be a guest performer at a concert the band was giving the following week. Louis did not hesitate with his reply.

The following is from a July 1945 issue of *Stars and Stripes*.

Bamberg DP Camp, Bamberg, Germany

Last nigh's program featured the First Battalion Band led by Lt. Murphy. The featured attraction was that man Louis Bannet, who really gives out with music. Have you heard Louis Bannet play that trumpet? Personally, he rates with the best in America. And when he starts playing that violin in jazz and opera, and his antics and clowning, he's really the best I've seen in a long time.

What the reviewer described as antics and clowning was Louis playing the violin upside down and behind his back, a trick he had learned from a Gypsy violinist in Auschwitz-Birkenau.

During the performance, Louis addressed the audience in several different languages, including perfect German. This caught the attention of an American major, a man ironically named Holland, who was a member of the new Counter-Intelligence Corps (CIC) in Bamberg. He asked to meet Louis as soon as possible.

For the thousands of Jewish refugees in Bamberg, the fate of family members was a lingering question, one to which they seemed to know the awful answer. Louis Bannet hadn't seen or heard from anyone in his family since he went into hiding, except his brother Isaac, whom he had left covered in waste in a hospital bed in Birkenau. It was a Dutch Jewish relief worker who told Louis the fate of his family. His brother Eduard and his two sons, his sister-in-law and her daughter, his brother Isaac's daughter, his brother Jacob's wife and daughter, his sister Cato and her two sons, his sister Beb and her four sons had all died in Auschwitz. One can only wonder if they heard Louis and the orchestra play as they were led to their deaths. Louis' mother Leentje died in Sobibor. He also learned that his father had died in a hospital in 1943. Remarkably, Louis discovered that his brother Isaac, whom he had rescued in Birkenau, had survived, as had his older brother Jacob, who had fled to Switzerland.

Several days later, Louis met Major Holland at CIC headquarters. In the early post-war days, the Counter-Intelligence Corps was heavily involved with the 'de-Nazification' process to clear people for possible employment as well as identify and apprehend war criminals. It was only later, as the Cold War escalated, that they became more involved with their classical function of identifying and apprehending spies.

Major Holland told Louis how much he had enjoyed his performance, and how glad he was that he had accepted Lieutenant Murphy's invitation to play with the First Battalion Band. He told Louis he had another offer him.

'I understand you speak fluent German,' the major said.

'Ja,' Louis answered.

'How would you like to help us catch some Nazis?' the major asked, as he took a bottle of bourbon from his desk and poured himself a glass.

Louis didn't have to think too hard before he answered.

'Yes. This I would like to do,' he said.

The next day, Louis Bannet, formerly prisoner 93626 of Auschwitz-Birkenau, became Corporal Louis Bannet. He was sworn in as a member of CIC Detachment 970/6 and issued with an American army uniform, a pistol, and a jeep.

His first assignment was to find and bring in an SS officer named Anton Orttel, who was said to be living in the nearby town of Scheinfeld. He was wanted for signing the deportation orders of thousands of children and elderly German Jews from hospitals in Germany. Louis was joined on this initial mission by a fellow Dutchman named Jan Dompselaar. They drove to Scheinfeld and found the home of the SS officer. Louis and Jan walked up to the front the house and knocked on the door. A young boy of about twelve came to the door. Louis spoke to the boy in German, asking him to get his father. The boy ran into the house. Soon a man appeared at the door.

'Are you Anton Orttel?' Louis asked in German.

'Yes, I am,' he replied.

'I have been ordered to bring you in for questioning. Please get your coat and come with us,' Louis said sternly.

'What is this about?' he asked Louis.

'You'll find out soon enough,' Louis replied.

Jan and Louis drove Orttel back to Bamberg. When Louis entered CIC headquarters, Major Holland was sitting at his desk, visibly intoxicated. Jan stayed to steady him, as Louis took Orttel to the second-floor interrogation room. Inside the room were a table and two chairs. Louis told Orttel to sit down, as he opened an envelope and took out several papers.

'You are Anton Orttel and you are an SS officer,' Louis said emphatically.

'Yes, that is my name, but I am not an SS officer. I was simply a soldier,' he replied.

'According to these papers, you sent thousands of old people and children, little babies, to die in the gas chambers,' Louis said as his voice broke in anger.

'I was simply a soldier,' Orttel flatly replied.

'Is this your signature on these deportation papers?' Louis asked, waving the papers in front of his face.

'I was simply a soldier,' Orttel answered, not even looking at the papers.

'You were simply a soldier. I see,' Louis said calmly.

'Please take off your coat,' he ordered. Orttel nervously removed his coat.

'Now I want you to remove your shirt,' Louis said.

'What kind of question is this?' Orttel shouted out.

'Remove your shirt, or I will rip it from your back,' Louis angrily shot back.

Orttel unbuttoned his shirt, slipped it off and sat with his arms folded.

'Now, lift up your arms,' Louis asked.

'What kind of game are you playing?' Orttel asked defiantly.

'Raise your arms now,' Louis demanded.

Orttel slowly lifted his arms into the air, revealing the tattoo every SS officer wore for life.

'So you were simply a soldier,' Louis said, as he glared at the man with his arms raised in the air. Louis then removed his pistol from its holster and placed it in the middle of the table.

'You are such a hero, aren't you? Sending old people and babies to burn in the ovens. If you are such a hero, why don't you take that gun in front of you and shoot me?' Louis asked. Orttel didn't know what to make of Louis' style of interrogation, and shook nervously in his chair.

'What's the matter, hero, don't you know how to use a gun? Here, I'll show you.' Louis reached for the gun on the table and shot Orttel. Jan and an American soldier came running up the stairs. They pushed open the door and saw Louis standing over the body of the SS officer.

'What happened?' the soldier asked.

'I was questioning him and he tried to grab my gun, so I had to shoot him,' Louis said. The soldier looked at the body slumped on the floor, walked over to Louis and took the pistol from his hand.

'Damn right you did,' the soldier said.

When Louis Bannet told me this story in Toronto more than fifty years later, he made me promise not to reveal it to anyone until he had passed away. He explained his actions this way:

'I looked at this man and thought: "This is the man who killed my family."'

That was Louis Bannet's first and last mission as a Nazi hunter. The next day, Major Holland gave Louis and Jan a seven-day furlough, and the two Dutchmen, dressed in their American uniforms, took off in their Jeep and headed back to Holland.

12. Picking Up the Pieces

After five years of brutal occupation, Allied forces captured Arnhem, Holland, in April of 1945. The remaining German forces surrendered on 4 May. The war had taken a terrible toll on Holland and the Dutch people, but perhaps no people were as devastated as the Dutch Jewish population. The Germans had deported more than 110,000 Jews out of Holland, but only some 5,000 survived to return. All in all, 35,000 Jews survived the war; 105,000 did not. This was the single biggest loss of Jews in any Nazi-occupied country in Western Europe. Jewish life, once so vital in Holland, has yet to recover, and most likely never will. Hitler may have lost his war against the Jews, but in Holland he did score a victory.

Jan Dompselaar knew Louis Bannet was not just without a home, but without a family, so he invited him to stay with his parents in Amersfroot. It would turn out to be a very worthwhile stay. One night, Jan's family organized a dinner at their home. They invited many of Jan's friends and their families. One guest was a beautiful young woman named Floortje Sarfaty. She had been hidden during the war, but her husband had perished in Buchenwald. More than fifty years later, when Canadian television was putting together a documentary on the life of Louis Bannet, archival footage of the camps was used. In one piece of film, Flora actually recognized the face of her husband in the crowded huddle of prisoners. In that documentary, you can also hear Louis' first impressions on seeing Floortje for the first time. 'She was the first Jewish woman I saw who was in good shape,' he recalled. She, of course, knew who he was. She and her husband, like so many other couples, had danced to his music in the nightclubs of Amsterdam. But now they were both without partners – survivors, with no one to turn to but each other. This was a bond even stronger than love, and after just two days, Louis and Flora (the name he called her) agreed to marry, vowing never to be alone again.

Louis and Flora eventually settled into a small apartment in Amsterdam. They had very little money and just a few possessions.

But Louis had two things no one could take away: his name and his talent. Music had saved his life before the war and during the war, and now he would use it to rebuild a life for himself and his new wife.

In the autumn of 1945, Louis reunited with Maurits von Kleef and bass player Jac de Vries and together they decided to re-form the Rhythm Five. They were the only surviving members, so two new members are recruited. After several weeks of intense rehearsals, Louis Bannet and the new Rhythm Five opened at the famous Savoy Club in Amsterdam. That night in December, the Savoy was filled with people hungry for a chance to laugh, to dance, to hold someone for the first time, not in the grip of fear, but with warmth and affection. At 8 p.m., Louis Bannet walked out on stage for the first time in nearly five years. By now, the Dutch papers had told the story of his survival, and of Maurits' and Jac's experiences. They were greeted with thunderous applause. Standing in the crowd, unable to hold back her tears, was Flora. Right beside her were Louis' closest friends, Peiter Dolk and Jan Dompselaar. Louis eyed them from the stage and smiled affectionately. As he had done so many times before, Louis looked back at Maurits, nodded his head, and once again began to play. The engagement was a huge success, and Louis Bannet and his Rhythm Five were held over for three months.

But for Maurits and Jac, the roar of the crowds couldn't quiet the pain of losing wives and children in the camps, and after the engagement at the Savoy, they told Louis this would be their last performance. Maurits eventually remarried and opened a women's clothing store in The Hague. Jac de Vries also started a new family and settled in Belgium. Louis remained in Amsterdam, unsure what his next move would be.

One day in the autumn of 1946, Flora answered a knock on the door. A young woman nervously asked to see Mr Louis Bannet. Flora told her that her husband was resting, and asked if she could come back a little later. The young woman told Flora that she had come a long way, so Flora invited her in, and asked her to wait in the parlor.

'Louis, you have a visitor,' Flora whispered, gently nudging her husband.

'A visitor? Who is it?' he asked.

'It's a young woman,' Flora said. 'She says she's come a long way to see you.'

'A fan, I suppose,', Louis said. Tell her I'll be out in a minute.'

'I'll bring you both some tea,' Flora said.

Louis walked into the parlor to greet his guest. The young woman stared at Louis intently.

'Good afternoon,' Louis said warmly. 'You'll have to forgive my napping. Musicians work very late, and we like to sleep during the day. What can I do for you?'

'Do you not remember me, Louis?' the woman asked.

'I play for so many people and I don't get to meet them all,' he answered.

'You played for me during the war,' she told him.

'In the DP camp? he asked.

'No, in Auschwitz,' she answered.

The woman slowly began to roll up her sleeve and revealed a name written on her arm. It was Louis' name.

'Oh my God, it can't be,' Louis said, his eyes fixed on the young woman's arm. 'Anita!'

Louis embraced the young Gypsy woman, as they both began to weep.

'How did you survive?' Louis asked. 'We heard all the Gypsies were killed.'

'Yes, all the Gypsies were killed, my father and brothers among them. But when they came for us that night, some of us were able to hide. When we were found, for some reason they didn't kill us, they just sent us to another camp. That's where I stayed until the end of war. Then I went back to Germany. I even married a German. Can you believe that, Louis?'

'But why did you keep my name on your arm?' Louis asked.

'I thought that one day I would be able to thank you. The last few weeks in the camp, when you came each day to play music, those few hours brought happiness to my family. It would be the last they would ever have. Do you remember that day, after the concert, when you told me the Germans were going to kill everyone that night? At first I didn't believe you, but some in the camp did, so I went with them and hid. Tell me, Louis, do you still play the music of my people?'

'I haven't it played it for many years,' he said.

'You once played it very well,' Anita said. 'Like a true Gypsy.'

Louis' experience with the Gypsies in Auschwitz had left an indelible mark on his life.

During an interview session in Toronto, he told my partner Jeroen and me that in all the years of playing and performing, he had written only one song, a song he had never played for anyone. He then reached into a drawer and removed a worn-out piece of paper. On it were the music and lyrics to a song called *Puszta*, the name used to describe the arid grasslands once so prevalent in Hungary. We asked him to play it for us, and he picked up his violin and played a lovely Gypsy melody. The lyrics are as follows:

> *In the Puszta I would like to live*
> *I want to dream of music*
> *Then I'll think of the melodies of the long-gone days of music*
> *And always do I hear the song in my ears*
> *The song of the Puszta I'll never forget*
> *Then I think of the long gone days of love and music*
> *I'll never forget*
> *The most beautiful thing on earth is music, music, music.*

Anita's visit must have had another impact on Louis because, over the next ten years, not only did he resume playing the music of the Gypsies, he lived like one. It all started with a call from a childhood friend. In the Helmerstraat, one of his closest friends was a boy with the voice of an angel. His name was Lazarus Fuld. He had attended the Amsterdam Jewish Seminary, where his unique talent was discovered, and by the time he was sixteen he was singing in synagogues all over Holland. But like Al Jolson in *The Jazz Singer*, Lazaraus was torn between the music of the nightclubs and the psalms of the temple, and his career as a cantor came to a close. His voice was far from silenced, however. Lazarus Fuld, now Leo Fuld, went to London as the singer for the popular Jack Hylton Orchestra, and at eighteen, he became the first Dutch singer to perform on the BBC. From there he went to New York, where he recorded the song that earned him the title King of Yiddish Music', *My Yiddishe Mama*. He eventually returned to Holland, but two months before the German invasion, Leo Fuld left for a tour of America. It would be last time he saw his family. Except for one sister, they all perished in the camps. When he called Louis to join him in 1949, it was the first time he had set foot in Holland since the war. Louis and Leo, the two childhood prodigies from the streets of Rotterdam, embarked on a three-month tour of Europe that took them to France, Belgium, Switzerland, and Germany. After the tour, Leo was booked for shows in America. He tried to get Louis to come with him, but the necessary paperwork never came through and Louis remained in Holland.

In August of 1951, a new sound was heard in the Bannet home, although it didn't emanate from a violin or trumpet. It was the cry of a baby, as Louis Bannet Jr. came into the world, nearly six years to the day of his father's liberation. When Louis held his son for the first time, he said, he truly felt free.

Though it was hard to leave Flora and Louis Jr., touring was the only way Louis could support his new family. In May of 1953, Louis was asked to play for Canadian forces in Halifax. Louis fell in love with Canada and the Canadian soldiers at Camp Utopia. He joined the Canadian army and was given the rank of staff sergeant, and he became a member of the famed Royal Canadian Band. He was also appointed to the violin and trumpet department of the Maritime Conservatory of Music. One of his greatest admirers was the base commander, General Allard, a burly French Canadian from Quebec, who loved to hear Louis play *Fascination* on the violin. When the troops were preparing to ship out for Korea, the general insisted that Louis accompany them as a member of the Royal Canadian Artillery Band. In a span of less than eight years, Louis had gone from being a prisoner of the Third Reich to a member of the US and Canadian armies.

Louis stayed in Korea for several months, playing French songs for the Canadian forces, and Gypsy melodies for the South Korean army. Before Louis left for home, General Allard told him of a friend who managed the famous Queen Elizabeth Hotel in Montreal. He offered to give Louis the highest recommendation should he decide to come to Canada. But all Louis could think of was getting back to Flora and his son. Canada seemed very far away.

In 1955, Louis, Flora, and Louis Jr. settled into a new apartment in The Hague. At the time, Louis was playing with Florian Zaback, a Hungarian vibraphone player. One of the songs they played in their show was a comical number called *Hot Canary*, a tune popularized many years before by the great jazz violinist Joe Venuti. Louis played the melody on the high notes of his violin, skipping his bow across the strings, imitating the sound of a singing canary. The performance never failed to bring the audience to its feet.

The next year, Russian tanks rolled into Hungary. Florian Zaback, fearing for his family's safety, returned to Budapest in an attempt to spirit them out of the country. Louis never heard from him again. Fearing that another war in Europe was imminent, Louis and his family decided to leave Holland and sailed for a new home and a new life in Canada.

13. Mon Coeur Est Un Violon

Louis' life in Canada began on a high note. Just two weeks after his arrival in April 1957, he was booked into the famous Chateau Frontenac in Quebec City. In the main ballroom he led the dance orchestra, playing both violin and trumpet. In between sets, he brought back his Louis Armstrong repertoire, ending each performance with *St. Louis Blues*.

One night Louis was visited in his dressing room by the legendary French singer Edith Piaf. She was so captivated by his story and performance that she invited him to play with her on stage. Louis offered to write a special arrangement of her signature song, *La Vie en Rose*, just for the occasion. A few nights later at her sold-out show, Piaf brought Louis on stage for her finale. Luckily, the evening's performance was recorded. I remember hearing it for the first time in Louis' home in Toronto. It is a beautiful, lush arrangement, marked by Louis' pizzicato playing. As the song draws to a close, Piaf sings the final refrain in English:

> *Give your heart and soul to me*
> *And life will always be*
> *La vie en rose*

Louis then repeats the refrain on the violin, and there's a pause, as Piaf turns to Louis and blows a very audible kiss. Sitting in his brown leather recliner, more than forty years later, Louis brushed his cheek as if the kiss had just landed.

In 1961, Louis was asked to open the new Salle Bonaventure of the glamorous Queen Elizabeth Hotel in Montreal. The engagement lasted four and a half years. For many young couples in Montreal, dancing to the music of Louis Bannet became a tradition. Many have said it was a common sight to see young men on one knee proposing to their girlfriends as Louis Bannet's music played. While at the Queen Elizabeth, Louis performed with such personalities as Rowan and Martin, Jane

Morgan, Nelson Eddy, Liberace, and Lawrence Welk. It was during this period that Louis' Bannet became known for the song *Mon Coeur Est Un Violon*, My Heart is a Violin. It would become his new theme song.

We know how Louis spent his nights in Montreal. The following piece from the *Montreal Gazette* gives a good idea how spent his days.

> To delight the ladies, The Queen Elizabeth, in cooperation with Eaton's of Canada, has introduced a regularly weekly 'Fashions at Luncheon' program in the Salle Bonaventure. Every Tuesday and Thursday at 12:45. Ladies lunching in this elegant dining room are treated to a showing of high style, late day and evening ensembles fashioned by designers of international fame. In this glamorous setting, with good food and delightful music provided by the popular Louis Bannet and his Trio, the models thread their way from the stage down through the dining room to give guests a close-up view of the latest fashions.

This gig didn't do much to advance Louis' career, but it did wonders for Flora's wardrobe.

Louis' popularity in Montreal didn't go unnoticed. The Gillette company was looking for a summer replacement show to fill some time in their schedule on Montreal's Channel 10. They offered Louis a contract for the summer season. Louis didn't know the first thing about this new contraption called television. But he did know what audiences liked to hear, and, in June 1964, *Mon Coeur Est Un Violon* made its debut.

> Madames and Monsieurs, Channel 10 in Montreal and The Gillette Shaving Company, makers of the Gillette Double-Edged Razor, is proud to present to you *Mon Coeur Est Un Violon* featuring the beautiful melodies of Louis Bannet.

The show consisted mostly of Louis, dressed in a tuxedo, playing his violin and trumpet into the camera. By the third week though, Louis felt the show needed a lift, and he thought a certain little bird could do the trick. He asked the prop man to find him a birdcage and a fake canary. During rehearsal, he had the director light the birdcage in silhouette. He attached a thin piece of wire to the fake bird, and asked a stagehand to move the bird as he played his violin. That night, in front of a live audience, and tens of thousands watching at home, Louis unveiled his trained canary act. As he played the cartoon-like tune *Hot Canary*, the bird moved its tiny feet in step to the music. The audience thought the bird was real and was actually dancing to the music. The feature made the show a huge hit, and Louis eventually made a recording of *Hot Canary* that went straight to number one. One of the musicians who played with Louis on *Mon Coeur Est Un Violon* was guitarist Buck Lacombe. His answer as to why the show was so popular was simple. He said Louis was a salesman of music. When he looked into the camera, he wasn't just playing: he was selling. Louis Bannet eventually recorded seventeen albums that featured everything from jazz to Hungarian folk songs to Christmas carols. One of Louis' favorite albums was called *Autour du Monde*, and it featured a collection of music that neatly summed up his musical journey. The songs on the album include *My Yiddishe Momma*, *Romanian Rhapsody*, *Stardust*, *Midnight In Moscow*, *Les Yeux Noirs* (Dark Eyes), and, of course, *St. Louis Blues*.

The television show *Mon Coeur Est Un Violon* ran for five seasons. Sadly, none of the shows was preserved. They remain part of Canada's early television history, with one important footnote: it is perhaps the only television show ever to be hosted by a Holocaust survivor.

The years that followed took Louis Bannet all over North America, from New York to the Canadian Rockies, where he played several summer seasons at the magnificent Jasper Park Lodge. Here he performed for royalty and Hollywood legends, such as Bob Hope and Bing Crosby. Louis said it was his favorite place to play. As the following letter attests, the feeling was mutual:

To whom it may concern.

I take great pleasure in writing this letter of recommendation for Mr. Louis Bannet who has been with us for the summer season. And whose professional services are very much appreciated both by guests and management alike. Mr. Bannet's approach to music make him an asset to us and we certainly look forward to many more years of a mutually beneficial relationship.

Yours truly, Henry Leland, General manager, Jasper Park Lodge, Alberta, Canada.

While in New York to play the Plaza Hotel, Louis got an urgent call from his old friend Leo Fuld, who was running the Sabbra, a sort of Jewish Copacabana, and at the time America's only Israeli-style nightclub. One of Leo's star performers fell ill and asked Louis to step in. Here's what the *New York Daily News* said about Louis Bannet's performance:

> To celebrate the fifth anniversary of the Sabbra, Leo Fuld has departed from the wailing wall type of entertainment and has brought a completely happy format to the club. The big surprise was the trumpeting of orchestra leader Louis Bannet, who gave his interpretation of the standard 'Ciribiribim.' Bannet, who spent three years in Auschwitz received a standing and whistling ovation for his rendition.

In the late 1970s, Louis and Flora followed their son Louis Jr. and his young family to Toronto, where Louis kept the promise he made to his Uncle Abraham so many years ago, and began to teach the violin to a small group of students. He also often spoke to schoolchildren about his experiences during the war.

One afternoon in the early 1980s, Louis was at home, napping in his study, when he was awoken by the telephone. The voice at the other end introduced himself as Henry Meyer. At first Louis couldn't place the name, but then Meyer mentioned that, as a young boy, he had played in the orchestra at Birkenau. Louis thought for a moment, and then remembered the tall, skinny kid who played the cymbals. Meyer told Louis that he was in Toronto on business and just happened to be calling from the airport. Louis told him to wait and he would pick him up in his car. When the two former band members met inside the terminal, they embraced like long-lost brothers. On the ride into the city they tried to catch up on the last fifty years. As they approached the city center, Henry Meyer took a cassette tape from his coat pocket.

'Louis, would you like to hear me play?' Meyer asked.

'Of course I would,' Louis replied.

Meyer handed Louis the tape. There was a brief moment of silence, and then the music of Beethoven, played by a string quarter, filled the car.

'This is you?' Louis exclaimed.

'This is the La Salle String Quartet, of which I am a member,' Meyer said proudly.

'So you're not a cymbal player,' Louis said.

'I was a cymbal player only because there was no space for another violinist in the Birkenau Orchestra,' Meyer answered. 'Before the war, I played violin at concert halls all over Germany. When I arrived at Birkenau, a German officer who had seen me play sent me to the orchestra. I told the capo that I could play the cymbals, even though I had never held a pair in my life. Do you remember how the soldiers used to throw stones at me, and I would have to catch them in my cymbals? I'm not sure which saved my life, my playing or my catching.' As the music ended, Louis reached into the glove compartment and removed a tape.

'Would you like to hear me play?' Louis asked.

'It would be an honor,' said Meyer. Louis put the tape in, and out poured the rousing Gypsy melody *Les Yeux Noirs*, played on the violin. Meyer was taken aback.

'I thought you played the trumpet,' Meyer said.

'I played it to save my life,' Louis replied.

Epilogue

In the early 1990s Louis Bannet walked into the office of Dr Steve Samuel, an eminent plastic surgeon in Toronto. He told the doctor that he wished to have something removed. Dr Samuel took a quick look at Louis, but didn't see any moles or scars. Louis rolled up his left shirt sleeve and asked the doctor to remove the numbers from his arm. Dr Samuel, himself the son of Holocaust survivors, spoke to Louis about the gravity of this decision. Louis said he would think it over. He thought about it for an entire year, and then returned to have the numbers 93626 permanently removed. When the procedure was over, Louis collapsed into the arms of Dr Samuel and they both wept. The numbers were gone, but they would never be erased.

In the autumn of 2000, Louis Bannet was diagnosed with lung cancer. After several months of aggressive chemotherapy treatments, the cancer went into remission. But even as he continued to give violin lessons and take Flora on her weekly shopping trips, it was obvious that the treatments had taken a toll on his strength and energy.

In April of that year, the long-running Canadian television news magazine *The W-Five* produced a feature story on the life of Louis Bannet. How fitting, I thought, that this story should appear as the world was celebrating the centenary of the birth of Louis Armstrong. I remember watching the show with my partner Jeroen, Louis and Flora and their friends and family in Toronto the night of its premier. Louis said it felt like opening night at Heck's Café. His performance in the piece captures the power, the warmth and enchantment of his personality. Most of all, the show bore witness not just to the horrors of the Holocaust, but to a truly beautiful love story, the story of Louis and Flora. When the interviewer tells Louis that she's heard that trumpet players make great kissers, Louis instantly turns to Flora, who, without missing a beat, nods a very emphatic yes. Flora also said that a day didn't go by when Louis didn't say 'I love you.'

I recall visiting Louis and Flora one August day in the summer of 2000. Louis had just turned ninety and he was preparing to take his driver's test to renew his license. When Flora greeted me at the elevator, she was visibly upset. It seemed Louis had been up all night studying for his test. I walked into the living room, where Louis was sitting on his beige leather recliner studying a stack of three-by-five index cards. He told me how nervous he was about the test. He talked about how a car meant freedom. The freedom to shop, visit friends and family, not to be trapped in the house. I thought it quite strange that a man who had once had to audition for his life was nervous about taking a driver's test. In writing this story, I have always been amazed by the similarities in some of Louis' experiences throughout his life. For example, when the young Louis walked into Bommel's Music Store in Rotterdam and came face to face with a wall of musical instruments, I couldn't help but compare that to the wall of instruments he saw in the *Muzikstube* in Birkenau. A similar feeling came over me when Louis told me about his driving test results a few days later.

When he went to take the test, he was asked to stand in line behind two older gentlemen who seemed nervous. The two men took the test and failed. Louis took his test and achieved a perfect score. I couldn't help but conjure the image of Louis at his audition in Birkenau watching the two Dutch musicians failing to play their instruments and being led away. Of course the consequences were very different, but even at the age of ninety, Louis still had the ability to pass every test placed before him.

In June of 2002, cancer and pneumonia finally accomplished what the Nazis could never do. Louis' final wish was to be cremated. Flora put his ashes in a Delft ceramic jar and placed it on a shelf next to his photograph; alongside she also placed a portable cassette player. Each morning she reaches up with her hand and affectionately taps the blue jar and speaks to Louis while his music plays. Louis Bannet, who once played for his life, now plays for Flora's.

Bibliography

Anderson, Anthony, *Anne Frank was not Alone: Holland and the Holocaust*, htttp://www-lib.usc.edu/~anthonya/holo.htm, 1995.

Czech, Danuta, Auschwitz Chronicle: *From the Archives of the Auschwitz Memorial and the German Federal Archives*, New York: Henry Holt, 1990.

Gilbert, Martin, *Atlas of the Holocaust*, New York: William Morrow, 1993.

Gutman, Yisrael and Michael Berenbaum (eds), *Anatomy of the Auschwitz Death Camp*, Bloomington: Indiana University Press, 1994.

de Jong, Louis, *The Netherlands and Nazi Germany*, Cambridge, MA: Harvard University Press.

Kater, Michael, *Different Drummers: Jazz in the Culture of Nazi Germany*, New York: Oxford University Press, 1992.

Presser, Jacob, *The Destruction of the Dutch Jews*, New York: E.P. Dutton, 1969.

Zwerin, Mike, *La Tristesse de Saint Louis: Jazz Under the Nazis*, New York: Beech Tree Books, 1987.